THE ESSENCE OF THE QURAN

COMMENTARY AND INTERPRETATION OF

SURAH AL~FATIHAH

ABDUL BASIT

ABC INTERNATIONAL GROUP, INC.

ii Essence of the Quran: surah al-fatihah

© 1997 Abdul Basit

All rights reserved. No part of this book may be reproduced or utilized in any form or by any means, electronic or mechanical, including photocopying and recording or by any information storage and retrieval system, without the written permission of the publisher.

Library of Congress Cataloging in Publication Data

Basit, Abdul
   The Essence of the Quran: surah al-fatihah

   Includes bibliographical references.
   1. Islam, Prayer. 2. Interpretation and Commentary.
   I. Basit, Abdul.   II. Title

ISBN: 1-871031-55-9

Published by
ABC International Group, Inc.

Distributed by
KAZI Publications
3023 W. Belmont Ave
Chicago IL 60618
Tel: 773-267-7001; (FAX) 773-267-7002
email: kazibooks@kazi.org

All that is contained in the revealed books
is to be found in the Quran,
and all that is contained in the Quran,
is summed up in the *surah al-fatihah*
— Prophet Muhammad

Contents

Preface	vii
Acknowledgements	xi
Introduction	1
First Verse: *Praise Be to God, Lord of the Worlds*	7
Second Verse: *Most Gracious, Most Merciful*	17
Third Verse: *Master of the Day of Judgment*	27
Fourth Verse: *Thee (Alone) We Worship,* *Thee (Alone) We Ask for Help*	41
Fifth Verse: *Show Us the Straight Path*	49
Sixth Verse: *The Path of Those Whom Thou Hast Favored*	61
Seventh Verse: *Not (the Path) of Those Who Earn Thine Anger* *Nor of Those Who Go Astray*	71
Notes	79
Bibliography	81
Index	83

Preface

I first began writing the commentary and interpretation of the Opening Chapter of the Quran(*surah al-fatihah*) in 1986, but then the administrative responsibilities as Superintendent of a mental hospital in the Chicago area lay heavily on my shoulders. Despite many attempts to complete the project, it was interrupted and postponed for one reason or another. In 1995 when I received my appointment as Assistant Professor of Clinical Psychiatry at the University of Chicago, the maddening pressure dissipated and the atmosphere suddenly became purely academic. After a few months, I was able to direct my attention toward the completion of this project. It took only a few months to finish the manuscript.

Many Muslim thinkers have attempted to explain the meaning and significance of the famous Opening Chapter. One of the most scholarly works was done by the late Maulana Abu 'l-Kalam Azad, first published in the Urdu language in 1931. Since it was a valuable contribution, it was highly acclaimed. It must, however, be stressed that since our ideas, thinking, and understanding of the world events and human behavior are largely shaped by the sociopolitical and religiocultural traditions of our time, a gap of more than half a century is enough time to bring major changes in the paradigm with which individuals perceive their world. Therefore, with all due deference to the late Maulana Azad, I have no hesitation in stating that the work produced here is the result of a completely different intellectual orientation.

Since I was born and raised in a family of eminent Muslim scholars in India, my early religious education left a perdurable impression. I received most of my formal education in Western universities, and for the past thirty-three years I have been living and working in either England or the United States. This extended exposure to Western religions, culture, and society has greatly expanded my horizons. Also, being an administrator, clinician, researcher, and university professor for more than thirty-three years, my objectivity is well-entrenched and my critical faculty is keenly sharpened. Consequently, my perceptions, interpretations, and explanations of many religious issues, concerns, and problems are thematically different.

During the past sixty-five years, the technological advances, scientific breakthroughs, and miracles of modern medicine have brought social changes at a rapid pace. Modern society, especially Western society, has been completely transformed. Unfortunately, the religious leaders have been so mesmerized by the minute details of arid rituals that they rigidly confine their message only to those areas. This undoubtedly diverted the attention from the main messages of the Quran—a guidance for the people [*huda 'l-nas*] and a cure for the sick soul.

In writing this book I have kept in mind that most of the readers will be Western-educated Muslims. Consequently, I have adopted a different, perhaps a more modern, approach, using language and symbols best suited to the mind and heart of the contemporary person. The readers, of course, will judge the results of this endeavor. My only hope is that this book will enable the readers to understand the fine and subtle nuances of the divine message that are beautifully contained in the seven wonderful verses of *surah al-fatihah*.

It should be noted that the use of blessings on Prophet Muhammad and other prophets and companions is common practice in Arabic, Persian, Turkish and Urdu, but this is not common practice in the English language. As this book is for both

English speaking Muslims and non-Muslims, and in order not to become too cumbersome for the non-Muslim reader, whether any indication is given after reference to their names or not, a Muslim would send blessings with his/her heart.

I wish to thank the members of the Halqa Muhammadi of Greater Chicago, who for the past seven years have been a source of inspiration. They have greatly appreciated my presentations at meetings of the Halqa and have provided constructive criticism. I also thank my younger brother, Mohammed Yunus, for his moral support and intellectual stimulation. I also gratefully acknowledge the help given by my talented daughter, Alia, who provided many worthwhile suggestions. Finally, I would like to thank my wife, Naheed. Her steadfast belief in my ability to complete this project was a continuing source of strength and inspiration.

I sincerely hope and pray that the God Almighty will bestow His blessings upon the author, and increase his understanding and knowledge of the Glorious Quran. Amin!

> Abdul Basit, Ph.D.
> Department of Psychiatry
> The University of Chicago
> June 1997

Acknowledgements

The author wishes to thank the following for permission to reproduce the quotations appearing in this book: Sachiko Murata and William C. Chittick, *The Vision of Islam*, St Paul, MN: Paragon House, 1994, and Karen Armstrong, *A History of God*, NY: Random House, Inc., 1993.

Introduction

Throughout the history of humankind devotional prayers have been offered to a higher deity in one form or another. Across the world, people petitioned the deity for aid with their material well-being. In ancient Chinese, Babylonian, Egyptian, Homeric, Indian, and Greek religions, prayers were essentially directed toward the attainment of temporal prosperity: they petitioned good health, rich progeny, and triumphant victory over their enemies. Ethical, moral, and spiritual prayer, beyond personal and material needs, developed later.

As religion became more spiritual and moral, the human being's prayer developed comparably. With the emergence of monotheistic religions a dramatic change was noted in the prayer. In the Pentateuch and the Gathas of the Avesta, which reflect the prophetic experiences of Moses and Zoroaster, the uncertainties of fear and doubt are overcome by the fear of hope and trust: creating a blissful comfort of being cared for by the infinite goodness of an Almighty and Omnipotent God. Higher forms of religion presented the notion of a higher deity and developed the notion of one God without any form or figure. The famous historian Edward Gibbon eloquently described this discursive process when he explained the Islamic idea of God.

> The prophet of Mecca [Muhammad] rejected the worship of idols and men, of stars and planets, on the rational principle that whatever rises must set, that

> whatever is born must die, that whatever is corruptible must decay and perish. In the author of the universe his rational enthusiasm confessed and adored an infinite and eternal being, without form or place, without issue or similitude, present to our most sacred thoughts, existing by the necessity of His own nature, and deriving from himself all moral and intellectual perfection.[1]

The idea of one God also emphasized that God, though infinite and beyond time and place, was nevertheless a personal God. The Biblical prophets continuously asserted that God was interested in providing divine guidance and help to people on Earth. In fact, prayer is based on the conviction that God exists, hears, guides, and answers—that He is a personal God. Consequently, most prayers offer petition, confession, adoration or thanksgiving to God; other types of prayer include invocation, supplication, intercession, penitence, and benediction.

When a person believes in a personal God, his prayer has the qualities of attention, devotion, and trust; he is really pouring out his heart before God. Though people around the globe with different historical and cultural backgrounds use different languages when praying to God, a common thread weaves them together: languages of prayer may be different but the tears are the same.

During the centuries one can see the six major categories of prayers: petition, confession, thanksgiving, praise, intercession, and penitence. Those of the petitions stated not only what was desired, but also the reason for the request. Penitential prayers confessed guilt and requested forgiveness and remission of punishment; often they also pleaded for deliverance from threatening danger. Prayer of thanksgiving for blessings received often included an admission of the human being's unworthiness to receive divine favors.

Prayer occupied a central position in the Jewish religion from the earliest days. The prayer of Israelites was deeply rooted in confidence in Yahweh's response. *"And it shall come to pass, that before they call, I will answer*" (Isaiah 65:24). There are many different forms of prayer in the Old Testament reflecting confession, thanksgiving, petition and intercession. On solemn occasions, however, the famous prayer, "*The Lord is my shepherd*," is recited.

> *The Lord is my shepherd; I shall not want. He maketh me to lie down in green pastures: he leadeth me beside the still waters. He restoreth my soul: he leadeth me in the path of righteousness for His name's sake. Yea though I shall walk through the valley of the shadow of death, I will fear no evil: for Thou art with me; Thy rod and Thy staff they comfort me. Thou preparest a table before me in the presence of mine enemies: Thou anointest my head with oil; my cup runneth over. Surely goodness and mercy shall follow me all the days of my life; and I will dwell in the house of the Lord forever* (Psalms 23:1-6).

Jesus is often mentioned in the New Testament as praying and instructing his followers to pray. He prayed publicly and privately before important decisions [Luke 3:31; Matthew 14:23]. He also taught his disciples how to pray: this prayer is now called the Lord's Prayer. And it is most frequently repeated by the Christians:

> *Our Father which art in heaven, hallowed be Thy name. Thy kingdom come. Thy will be done, as in heaven so in earth. Give us this day our daily bread, and forgive our sins, for we also forgive everyone that is indebted to us. And lead us not into temptation but deliver us from evil* (Matthew 6:9-13, Luke 11:2-5).

Nearly six hundred years after Jesus, the Arabian Prophet, Muhammad, re-established the monotheism of the patriarch Abraham in its purest form. He presented a universal idea of God. According to the Quran, God is the Lord of the worlds. He is a universal God. Though He is infinite and absolute, He is a personal God who is nearer to man *"than his jugular vein"* (50:16). The famous Muslim prayer, which is recited during worship five time a day, is called *surah al-fatihah*.

> *In the Name of God, Most Gracious, Most Merciful*
> *Praise be to God, Lord of the Worlds;*
> *Most Gracious, Most Merciful;*
> *Master of the Day of Judgment.*
> *Thee (alone) we worship; Thee (alone) we ask for help.*
> *Show us the straight path.*
> *The path of those whom Thou hast favored;*
> *Not (the path) of those who earn Thine anger nor of those who go astray.*

Surah al-fatihah or the Opening Chapter is actually the Lord's Prayer of the Muslims. It is recited in prayers five times a day and is an integral part of all Muslim worship. It is also one of the earliest chapters revealed, probably the first complete chapter revealed in the early days of the Prophet's mission. By general consent of the early Muslim scholars it is considered one of the most important chapters. According to the Prophet all that is contained in the revealed books is to be found in the Quran and all that is contained in the Quran, is summed up in the *surah al-fatihah*.

Consequently, many authentic Traditions [*ahadith*] state that *surah al-fatihah* has been called by the Prophet: Essence of the Quran (*umm al-quran*); Foundation of the Quran (a*ssas al-quran*); the Treasure (*al-kinz*); and Seven of the Oft-repeated (*saban min al-mathani*). The last name, *saban min al-mathani*, for *surah al-fatihah* is derived from the Noble Quran:

> *And we have bestowed upon thee the seven oft-repeated (verses) and the Grand Quran* (15:87).

In fact, these seven verses form a complete unit by themselves. This beautiful chapter is so thorough, comprehensive, and universal that in brief it contains the basic teachings of the Glorious Quran. Many Western scholars, even some Christian missionary workers, have been profoundly impressed by the universal characteristic and sublime style of the prayer.

The followers of the monotheistic religions, whether Jews or Christians, could all recite *surah al-fatihah* without any reservation. It is this universal aspect of the Lord's Prayer that has attracted the attention of many non-Muslim scholars.

Alfred Guillaume, a noted Islamic scholar, remarked:

> There is nothing in the official worship of Islam in which a Christian could not join, and one who understands the word of praise and adoration is tempted to do so.[2]

One Christian missionary writer was fascinated by the constant repetition of this prayer in all parts of the world.

> These seven verses [of *surah al-fatihah*] are the most recited words on Earth, because Muslims offer prayers daily five times and more than one in six of the world's population is Muslim.[3]

In this book, the author attempts to explain and interpret the meaning, significance, and importance of each of these seven verses that form the magnificent Opening Chapter.

FIRST VERSE:
PRAISE BE TO GOD, LORD OF THE WORLDS

In the first verse, which is the opening of the prayer, it is solemnly declared that all praise belongs to God, Who is Lord of the universe. Since it is a prayer, it is most befitting to start with the praise and adoration of God [*al-hamd*]. Although four other chapters [*anam, kahf, saba,* and *fatir*] also begin with *al-hamd*, their central themes are different. But *surah al-fatihah* is actually the Lord's Prayer, and therefore the only chapter where the central theme is an ejaculation of praise and thanksgiving [*tahmid*].

At the center and foundation of Islam is God. The Quran speaks of God in innumerable verses of great splendor and beauty, and this name, Allah, appears about 2,700 times in the text of the Quran. God is the name of the Essence or the Absolute. The word God in Arabic, Allah, is a contraction of two words, the article *"al"* and the word *"ilah"* [divinity]. The name Allah was known and used long before the emergence of Islam in Arabia. For example the name of the Prophet's father was "Abd Allah." The word Allah in Arabic language has always been used for one God, the Supreme Being.

It is worth special mention that the Arabic word "Allah" which sounds so alien to the Western world was used, with slight variation, in the Hebrew and Aramaic languages, long before

Prophet Muhammad. In the Old Testament the word "Elohim" is used quite often for God. When Jesus in extreme pain and agony cried for God, he used the word "Eli"(Matthew 27:46) or "Eloi" (Mark 15:34). Probably the origin of these words—"Elohim," "Eloi," Eli," and *"ilah"*—is found in a root common to the family of Semitic languages.

The use of the word Allah in English, however, has given many misleading impressions. When people hear the word Allah in English, many think that Allah is the god of the Muslims, just as Vishnu is the god of the Hindus, or Zeus was the god of the ancient Greeks. They therefore conclude that Jews and Christians believe in a different god—the real God.

But the word Allah in Arabic simply means God. The Quran, the *hadith*, and the whole Islamic literature consistently maintains that the God of the Jews, Christians, and the Muslims is one God. Even now the name Allah is not confined to Islam alone. When Arabic-speaking Christians and Jews worship God, they use the word "Allah." This confusion has been generated not only by English-speaking Christians and Jews, but also by narrow-minded Muslims. The Islamic scholars Murata and Chittick delineate this subtle point very well:

> Use of Allah in English is misleading in discussion of the first *shahadah*. If it is translated as 'There is no god but Allah,' this has a very different connotation from the sentence 'There is no god but God.' For example, it does not sound totally unreasonable to claim that Moses and Jesus taught that 'there is no god but God,' but it sounds ridiculous to say that they were preaching that 'There is no god but Allah.' English speakers unacquainted with Islam naturally tend to understand Allah to be some false, alien god of the same sort that pagan and other nonbeliever worship (whoever they might be).
>
> Some Muslims insist on using the word Allah when they speak English for several reasons. First, it is the primary name of God in the Koran, so the word itself is

considered to have a special blessing. Second, most Muslims who speak English are not native speakers of the language, and at the same time it is perfectly obvious to them that Islam is a true religion. Hence they cannot imagine the misunderstandings that arise in the minds of the non-Muslim, native speakers of English simply by the mention of the word Allah. Third, many Muslims have little grasp of the theology of their own religion. Hence they think that Allah is the true God, and the word God as used in English refers to a false god worshiped by Jews and Christians. Such Muslims represent the mirror image of those English speakers who think that God is the true God and Allah is a false god worshiped by pagans. [4]

The Quran, however, has repeatedly emphasized that the name of God is not really important. What is vitally important is the universal idea and unity of God.

> *Say (unto mankind) call upon God or call upon the Compassionate, by whatever name you call upon Him (it is the same). For to Him belongs the most beautiful Names* (17:110).

> *The most beautiful names belong to God so invoke Him by them* (7:180).

After stating that all praises are to God, the word "*rabb*" is used; Who is the Lord [*rabb*] of the worlds. In fact, the first revelation in the cave of Hira asks the Prophet to recite in the name of the Lord:

> *Recite in the name of thy Lord, who has created— created the human being out of a leech-like clot. Recite for thy Lord is the Most Bountiful* (96:1-3).

The Arabic word "*rabb*" is very comprehensive and usually

three distinctive meanings are ascribed to it: Master or Lord; Sustainer or Cherisher; and Sovereign or Judge. It is used when an individual in a state of desperation and helplessness is earnestly seeking God's help and guidance. Most supplications seeking God's grace, mercy, and forgiveness begin with the word Lord. A few examples are given below:

> *Our Lord! Give us good in this world and good in the Hereafter and save us from the torment of fire (2:201).*

> *Our Lord! Lay not on us a burden greater than we have strength to bear. Blot out our sins. And grant us forgiveness. Have mercy on us. Thou art our Protector; give us victory over the unbelievers (2:286).*

> *Our Lord! Cause not our hearts to stray after Thou hast guided us, and bestow upon us mercy from Thy Presence. Lo! Thou, only Thou art the Bestower (3:8).*

> *Our Lord! Forgive us our sins and anything that we may have done that transgressed our duty: Establish our feet firmly, and help us against those who resist faith (3:147).*

> *Our Lord! Accept from us (this duty). Lo! Thou, only Thou art the Hearer, the Knower. Our Lord! And make us submissive unto Thee, and our seed a nation submissive unto thee, and show us our ways of worship, and relent toward us. Lo! Thou, only Thou, art the Relenting, the Merciful (2:127-128).*

> *Our Lord! Perfect our light for us, and forgive us! Lo! Thou art able to do all things (66:8).*

This Sustainer, Sovereign, and Judge is Lord of the worlds

[*rabb al-alamin*]. By stating that God is Lord of the worlds, a universal concept of God is established at the very beginning. He is not the God of "Arabs" or "Israel" or "Aryans" or any particular tribe or nation. No! He is the Lord of all people—a universal God. Therefore, every place in which God is faithfully worshiped is equally pure. It is one of the glories of Islam that prayers can be performed anywhere upon God's earth.

Because of God's universality, the followers of Islam also belong to a community of universal brotherhood bound by a common faith and committed to the creation of an ideal society where all people, despite their color, national origin, social or political status, are equal. During the first seven years of the Meccan period, the Quran made fervent denunciation of social injustice, fraud, exploitation of the poor, and the mad craze for wealth. It was this accusation that the Quran constantly laid against the Quraysh that made the Quraysh furious.

Unfortunately Muslims have forgotten or grossly under emphasized this essential part of the Quranic teaching. In their zeal religious leaders have placed such a tremendous stress upon man's obligation and gratitude to God [*huquq* Allah] that concern for justice and violation of the basic human rights [*huquq al-ibad*] has been totally eclipsed. Even Western scholars of Islam agree that the Quran teaches a just and ethically-based social order which eliminates the exploitation of the poor and weak and where the equality of the human race is firmly established. According to Huston Smith:

> Its [Quran] moral teaching, demanded an end to the licentiousness which citizens were disinclined to give up; and its social content was dynamite to an effete and unjust economic order. In a society driven with class distinction, the new Prophet [Muhammad] was preaching a message intensely democratic, insisting that in the sight of his Lord all men are equal.[5]

From the very beginning, Islam tried to obliterate all distinction among people practiced in most societies. The Quran vehemently denounced discrimination of people based on race, color, social, and economic status:

> The noblest of you in the sight of God is the one most possessed of piety and righteousness [taqwa] (49:13).

The immense importance of this teaching can be judged by an incident that occasioned the revelation of the Quranic chapter "*abasa.*" In the early Meccan period, when the opposition was fierce and the converts few, the Prophet was eager to attract some influential Meccans who may be able to turn the tide. Fortunately a group of wealthy Meccan leaders came to see the Prophet to learn the new religion. While the Prophet was earnestly engaged in explaining the teachings of the Quran to the leaders, he was interrupted by Abd Allah ibn Umm al-Maktum, who was blind and poor. Abd Allah ibn Umm al-Maktum, who had already converted to Islam, wanted to learn more about the Quran. Though kindhearted by nature and always sympathizing with the poor and afflicted, the Prophet naturally did not like the interruption during his discourse with the Meccan leaders. But Ibn Umm al-Maktum, being blind, could not see the Prophet's face and kept asking questions. Since the Prophet seemed annoyed, Ibn Umm al-Maktum was probably hurt. Consequently, the Prophet was reproved by God.

> (The Prophet) frowned and turned away, because there came to him the blind man (interrupting). But what could tell thee but that perchance he might grow in purity? Or that he might receive admonition, and that reminder might profit him? As to one who regards himself as self-sufficient to him dost thou attend; though it is no blame to thee if he grow not in purity. But as to him who came to thee striving earnestly and

with fear (in his heart) of him wast thou unmindful. By no means (should it be so) for it is indeed a Message of remembrance (80:1-11).

It must also be emphasized that the Prophet and his Companions not only preached but strictly practiced this teaching. It was for this reason that the Prophet made a special point to emphasize this message during his famous Farewell Pilgrimage address:

> O ye people! Verily your Lord is one and your father is one. All of you belong to Adam and Adam was made of clay. An Arab has no superiority over a non-Arab, nor does a non-Arab have superiority over an Arab; nor a white have superiority over a black, nor a black have superiority over white. Verily the noblest among you is he who is most pious.

An in-depth study of the Quran reveals that belief in one universal God is the "anchor point" or the "master truth"—and without it nothing meaningful could be accomplished. Without this belief, the human being will relentlessly drift in a vast ocean of doubts and uncertainties. God is that "dimension that makes other dimensions possible." He gives meaning and life to everything. Belief in God cures one's sense of insecurity by bringing the individual into communion or union with the Supreme Being. It gives him hope in despair, shows him light in darkness, lifts depression when burdens are heavy, makes death bearable, and fills him with a spirit to crusade against evil.

When one achieves this "truth" and as it deepens into the psyche of the individual, one is free from all types of bondage, including the worship of people [*shirk*] who behave as "gods" because of their wealth, power, knowledge or influence. For a person who has complete faith in God, God is the only helper, the sole refuge.

One basic pitfall of human beings has been to take the various attributes of the one universal God and treat them as many gods. For example Zoroaster and his followers believed that there were two gods: Ahura Mazda and Ahriman, symbols of good and evil, who were engaged constantly in struggle. In the Hindu religion many gods are recognized and each god has his or her own function. Three principal gods are generally accepted, symbolizing creation, preservation, and destruction—the term used is three powers [*trimurti*]. And the devotees can worship the god which will meet their immediate needs. A similar idea is reflected in the Christian concept of the trinity: Father, Son, and the Holy Spirit.

Surprisingly enough the doctrine of the trinity, which later became a cornerstone of the Christian faith, is not at all mentioned in the New Testament. This term was used for the first time by the Latin theologian Tertullian in the 2nd century. Even in the early stages, there had been serious opposition to the idea of the trinity. Arius of Alexandria (d. 336 AD), a great Biblical scholar, stressed the essential difference between God and all His creatures. Well-versed in the scriptures Arius argued that God was the only eternal, the only one without beginning, the only true, the only one who has immortality, the only wise, the only good. Nevertheless, when Bishops gathered at Nicaea (325 AD) to resolve the issue, Arius was overruled by others. It was further crystallized in the 5th century by St. Augustine's famous work *De Trinitate*.

In all fairness, it must also be stated that many Christian scholars have made attempts to explain this doctrine of the trinity as a philosophical or abstract concept: God as entity, life, and knowledge. Still, the riddle of the trinity [three in one and one in three] has consistently plagued Christianity and this doctrine has sometimes been understood in concrete form also. For example, many Christian theologians firmly believed that the three persons of the trinity are, in effect, three gods. The view of Incarnation was best expressed by Anselm (d. 1109 AD) in his treatise, *"Why God Became Man."* In trying to explain the paradoxical nature of this doctrine of the trinity, it was suggested that the trinity is a mystery and one must accept it and not try to understand it. Armstrong summarized this aspect of the controversy:

> Ultimately, however, the Trinity only made sense as a mystical or spiritual experience: it had to be lived, not thought, because God went far beyond human concepts. It was not a logical or intellectual formulation but an imaginative paradigm that confounded reason. Gregory of Nazianzus made this clear when he explained that contemplation of the Three in One induced a profound and overwhelming emotion that confounded thought and intellectual clarity.[6]

As opposed to Christian doctrine, the Quran strictly maintains the concept of unity. There is only One God, and it is a grave error, rather a cardinal sin, to believe in many gods. The various attributes of God have often been mistakenly taken as various gods with specific characteristics. But these various attributes of God, according to the Quran, reflect the multifaceted nature of the One God.

The famous Chapter of Sincerity (*surah al-ikhlas*), which according to many authentic Traditions, contains the essential teaching of the Quran, calls God " the Eternal (*al-Samad*)."

> *Say: He is God, The One and Only. God the Eternal [al-Samad] and the Absolute. He begetteth not, nor is He begotten; and there is none Like unto Him* (112).

Though translation of "*al-Samad*" in English is difficult, the famous al-Jurjani of the Asharite school stated that the word *al Samad* implies "without mixture of any sort, without any possibility of division into parts, because in God there is no hollow."

The noted Islamic scholar Louis Massignon translated the word "*al-Samad*" as "dense to the absolute degree." The word also means "an immovable and indestructible rock without cracks or pores, which serves as sure refuge from floods." Consequently, various scholars of the Quran have translated *al-Samad* as: the Eternal and Absolute; the Uncaused Cause of all being; Eternally Besought of all; and the Everlasting Refuge.

Most of the universal attributes of God along with His power and majesty are best described in the following two passages of the Quran:

> *He is the God, other than Whom, there is none; the Knower of the invisible and the visible. He is the Beneficent, and the Merciful, He is God, other than Whom, there is none, the Sovereign Lord, the Holy One, Peace, Keeper of faith, the Guardian, the Majestic, the Compeller, the Superb. Glorified be God from all that they ascribe as partners (unto Him). He is God, the Creator, the Shaper out of naught, the Fashioner. His are the most beautiful names. All that is in the heavens and the earth glorifieth Him, and He is the Mighty, the Wise (59:22-24).*

> *God is the Light of the heavens and the earth. The parable of His light is, as if there were a niche and within it a lamp: the lamp enclosed in glass; the glass [shining] like a radiant star: Lit from a blessed Tree, an olive, neither of the East nor of the West, the oil whereof [is so bright that it] would well-nigh give light [of itself] even though fire had not touched it: Light upon Light (24:35).*

Second Verse:
Most Gracious, Most Merciful

The second verse brings out two other attributes of God: *"rahman"* and *"rahim."* The word *"rahman"* has been translated in English as "the Compassionate," "Most Gracious," or "the Beneficent." The word *"rahim"* means "the Merciful." Experts of the Arabic language have lengthy discourse describing the distinction between the word *"rahman"* and *"rahim."* But before this is addressed, it is important to note that the word *"rahman"* was for some reason unfamiliar to the Meccans. While they understood the word *"rahim,"* they seemed rather puzzled to hear the word *"rahman."* Even the Quran refers to this astonishment by the Meccans:

> *When it is said to them, 'Adore ye the Most Gracious [rahman],' they say, 'What is Most Gracious [rahman]? Shall we adore that which thou commandest us?' And it increases them in aversion (25:60).*

The use of the word *"rahman"* became controversial when the terms of the Hudaybiyyah Treaty were being written. When Suhayl, who was representing the Quraysh, finally agreed to the terms, the Prophet instructed Ali ibn Abi Talib to write down the treaty beginning with "In the Name of God, the Most Gracious, the Most Merciful" [*bismi llahi al-rahman al-rahim*]. Suhayl objected immediately and said, "As to *rahman*, I know not what he is. But write "In Your Name O God" [*bismi ka allahumma*].

18 Essence of the Quran: surah al-fatihah

However, both these divine epithets, the Most Gracious and the Most Merciful, are derived from the noun *"rahmah,"* which reflects mercy, compassion, loving tenderness, and grace. The great commentator of the Quran, al-Baydawi (d. 1291 AD), states that *al-Rahman* is a more exalted attribute than *al-Rahim* because the word *"rahman"* [Most Gracious] expresses the universal attribute of mercy that the Almighty extends to all people, the good and the bad, the believers and unbelievers.

The infinite bliss and mercy of God is manifested through the two dimensions: the static plenitude of *al-Rahman* and the dynamically redemptive and immanent plenitude of *al-Rahim*. Using these words one after another [*rahman* and *rahim*] accentuates the special attributes of *"rahmah"* in God. In other words, it reminds us that God's grace and mercy are in abundant measure for his creatures. His divine mercy and forgiveness are repeatedly emphasized in the Quran:

> *Say God has inscribed for Himself the rule of mercy* (6:12).

> *My (God) mercy embraceth all things* (7: 56).

> *We (God) are nearer to him than his jugular vein* (50:16).

The most often repeated attributes of God in the Quran, besides "the Most Merciful" [*al-Rahim*] and "the Most Gracious" [*al-Rahman*], are "the Returner" [*al-Tawwab*] and "the Forgiver" [*al-Ghafur*] which are almost invariably followed by the name Most Merciful (*rahim*):

> *For He is Oft-Returning, Most Merciful* (2:37, 2:54).

> *For I am oft-Returning Most Merciful* (2:160).

> *For God is Oft-Forgiving, Most Merciful* (2:173, 2:182, 5:39).

Second Verse: Most Gracious, Most Merciful   19

Though God is depicted as "Lord of Majesty" (55:78), the Quran emphasizes that He is the Giver, the Dispenser of all that is good, the Consenter, the Answerer, the Friend, and the Protector. Closely related with mercy is the Quranic concept of love (*hubb*). Love is a divine attribute: God is love. For reasons that we need not discuss here, theologians tend to avoid discussing the Quranic conception of God's love. But the Sufis presented the concept of love as the key to Islamic life and practice.

Of all the Sufis (Muslim mystics), Rumi (d. 1273 AD) is the greatest poet of love; to him, love is Islam's lifeblood, and without this the religion will dry up.

> Love is a boundless ocean, in which the heavens are but a flake of foam. Know that all the wheeling heavens are turned by waves of love: were it not for love, the world would be frozen (Rumi).

Consequently, Rumi never ceases to emphasize God's nearness and His love for human beings. The love of God is repeatedly mentioned in the Quran.

> *Do what is beautiful! Surely God loves those who do what is beautiful* (2:195).

> *Those who give alms both in ease and adversity and who restrain their anger and pardon people. God loves those who do what is beautiful* (3:134).

> *Whoso fulfills his covenant and is pious; surely God loves those who are pious* (3:76).

> *Truly God loves those who repent, and He loves those who cleanse themselves* (2:222).

> *Put thy trust in God. Lo! God loveth those who put their trust (in Him)* (3:159).

> And act equitably. Lo! God loveth the equitable (49:9).

> Truly God loves those who fight in His cause in battle array, as if they were a solid cemented structure (61:4).

In contrast, about twenty-three verses focus on those specific attitudes or behaviors that God does not love. One is not surprised to learn that God does not love those whose character and activities are not beautiful: those who are wrongdoers, corrupt, proud, transgressor, boastful, or greedy of possessions and riches.

> For God loveth not any vainglorious boaster (57:23).

> No indeed, but you honor not the orphan; and urge not on the feeding of the poor. And ye devour heritage with devouring greed, and love wealth with an ardent love (89:17-20).

> Made attractive to people is the love of things they crave—women, children, heaped-up heaps of gold and silver, horses of mark, cattle, and tillage. That is the enjoyment of the life of this world. But God—with Him is the beautiful homecoming (3:14).

The message is simple: people should not be led astray by the fleeting beauty that attracts the cravings of most people in this world. Nay! They should love the permanent beauty of God. How can people love God? They can move toward God through the right faith, good deeds, and doing what is beautiful.

God is indeed so merciful that if sinners sincerely repent, He will not only forgive their sins, but He will even transmute their lapses [*sayyiat*] into goodness [*hasanat*]:

> Save him who repenteth and believeth and doth

righteous work; as for such, God will change their evil deeds to good deeds. God is ever Forgiving, Merciful (25:70).

Since God is both Most Gracious, Most Merciful, His guidance for mankind [*huda li-nas*], revealed through the messengers in all ages to all nations, is called a sign of His "*rahmah.*" Both the message and the messengers are described as blessings springing from the fountain of God's boundless mercy.

If it were Our will, We could take away that which We have sent thee by inspiration. Then wouldst thou find none to plead thy affair in the matter as against Us except for mercy from thy Lord for His bounty is to thee (indeed) great (17:86-87).

It is revelation sent down by (Him), the exalted in Might, Most Merciful, in order that you mayest admonish a people, whose fathers had received no admonition, and who therefore remained heedless (of the signs of God) (36: 5-6).

Similarly other divine revelations were also due to His "*rahmah.*" The Noble Quran declares that the revelations given to other prophets before Muhammad were also due to His bounty and blessings. The book of Moses is therefore a guide and a mercy:

Can they be (like) those who accept a clear (sign) from their Lord and followed by a witness from Him, and before him is the book of Moses before it—a guide and a mercy? (11:17).

This final revelation, given to Prophet Muhammad, contains a prescription for healing the sick soul. This reflects the bounty of God and His everlasting mercy:

> *O mankind! there hath come to you a direction from your Lord and a healing for the (diseases) in your hearts and for those who believe a Guidance and a Mercy. Say: 'In the Bounty of God, and in His Mercy in that let them rejoice,' that is better than the (wealth) they hoard (10:57-58).*

Considering the limitless mercy of God, the Noble Quran wants its followers to inculcate this attribute of mercy in themselves. The Prophet also consistently tried to instill this virtue into his Companions. The Quran, therefore, calls the Prophet "mercy for mankind" [*rahmat al-alamin*] and encourages the followers to follow the Prophet's acts and deeds. One must use the life and character of the Prophet Muhammad as a model. The following verses of the Quran clearly stress this point:

> *We sent you [Muhammad] not, but as a mercy for all creatures (21:107).*

> *Say [O Muhammad to mankind]: if you love God, follow me, and God will love you and forgive you your sins. God is Forgiving, Merciful (3:31).*

If one reviews the life and character of the Prophet, it becomes abundantly clear why the Noble Quran is so emphatic in stating that one must follow his beautiful conduct:

> *We have indeed in the Messenger of God, a beautiful pattern (of conduct) for any one whose hope is in God and the Final Day (33: 21).*

Both Muslim and non-Muslim writers have produced a massive amount of work on the life and character [*sirah*] of the Prophet. Learned scholars all over the world have written hundreds of books on the life of the Prophet. Most Muslim authors have shrouded the Prophet's extraordinary dynamic personality in the mystery of miracles. Orientalists usually give a rather negative sketch of his life and those who tried to maintain an unbiased approach showed little appreciation for the outstanding achievements and accomplishments of Prophet Muhammad. Consequently most attempts, to some extent, obscured his exemplary conduct as a human being.

Never in the history of humankind has a person been born where so many different qualities were combined in one person. First, in contrast to other Prophets, we know a lot more about Prophet Muhammad. History records his family life, the emergence of Islam, the struggle against all odds to establish the Muslim community, failures and successes, victories and defeats, negotiations with the enemy and other parties, and many other events associated with the life of Prophet Muhammad. The divine revelation (called the Quran) was meticulously preserved in the same form and language as it was revealed. Still to this day—for both friends and foes—the Quran is an undisputed document in its original form.

Extensive records of the Prophet's sayings, acts, and deeds [sunna] were carefully kept. The Arabic language he spoke is still spoken by more than 220 million people in the world.

Not only do we know where he is buried, but we also know where most of his best companions are buried. Historical aspects of his life and character are real, available in detail for his followers to emulate in every walk of life.

Historians of the world have been baffled by the visionary side of Prophet Muhammad, his genius for handling complex problems, his immense power to capture people's minds and hearts, the universal aspect of his religion, and the invincible character of his early followers. In less than two decades, the solitary and persecuted preacher of Mecca established a new religion and set in motion one of the most remarkable revolutions that permanently changed the map and history of the world. The rapid speed with which Islam spread over the world is really amazing, especially when compared with other religions, such as Christianity and Judaism, which took centuries to evolve.

When measured by influence on succeeding generations, Prophet Muhammad ranks as one of the giants among world's religious leaders. According to the famous psychoanalyst, Jules Masserman:

> Leaders must fulfill three functions—provide for the well-being of the lead, provide a social organization in which people feel relatively secure, and provide them with one set of beliefs. . . . Perhaps the greatest leader of all times was Mohammad (*sic*), who combined all three functions. To a lesser degree, Moses did the same.[7]

Also Michael Hart, the author of the famous book, *The One Hundred Most Influential People in History*, after an in-depth review of world history, concluded that Prophet Muhammad was the greatest leader who immensely influenced the course of world history.[8]

During the twenty-three years of his prophetic life, Muhammad reflected different, varied, but distinguishable and extraordinary characteristics. No other person in the history of the world ever possessed such diverse and unmatched qualities. He was an orphan and poor, but became rich and prosperous. He was a lonely and persecuted preacher of Mecca, but later became prince of Medina. He was an unlettered and unschooled man who became the great teacher of Muslim community. He was a quite and peace-loving man who suddenly became one of the best military geniuses. He was never involved in the political circle of wealthy Quraysh, but became the greatest statesman of Arabia. He showed immeasurable patience and fortitude when facing bitter opposition and persecution; he exhibited fearless courage even in the face of grave dangers, he was defiant and undaunted when he faced defeat or setbacks. He was extremely honest and trustworthy earning the title of "the Trustworthy" [*al-amin*], and demonstrated unparalleled generosity and magnanimity to his enemies when total victory was achieved.

After becoming the leader of Medina, he was not only a

Prophet but a father, husband, administrator, commander-in-chief, lawgiver, and judge. Though he had access to a vast treasure of the world, he preferred to live a simple life. The Prophet, in fact, always viewed earthly phenomena in the light of eternity. This point is best illustrated by the famous author Karen Armstrong:

> Muhammad himself lived a simple and frugal life, even when he became the most powerful sayyid in Arabia. He hated luxury and there was often nothing to eat in his household. He never had more than one set of clothes at a time and when some of his Companions urged him to wear a richer ceremonial dress, he always refused, preferring the thick, coarse cloth worn by most of the people. When he received gifts and booty, he gave it always to the poor and , like Jesus, he used to tell the Muslims that the poor would enter the Kingdom of Heaven before the rich. It was no accident that many of his first converts were among the disadvantaged people of Mecca: slaves and women both recognized that this religion offered them a message of hope. As we shall see, he did attract converts from the richer clans, but most of the powerful and aristocratic Quraysh held aloof: when the Muslims gathered around the Kabah, they scoffed at the riff-raff with whom the grandson of the great Abdul al-Muttalib was pleased to associate. When Islam became more powerful, it was not the wealthier Muslims of the upper-class who were his closest companions but the more plebeian converts from the poorer clans of Quraysh. None of this was simply a matter of personal preference. Muhammad knew that he had to set an example to the first Muslims and that al-Llah hated injustice and exploitation. A decent society, that reflected God's will, must cultivate a strictly egalitarian way of life.[9]

Prophet Muhammad and his followers were mercilessly persecuted, relentlessly hounded for ten years in Mecca, and, finally, driven out of their native town. Even then the Meccans would not leave them alone. They continued to wage war with the sole purpose of annihilating the message and the messenger. In 630 AD, when the Muslims entered Mecca triumphantly, the proud and mortal foes of Prophet Muhammad were prostrate at his feet. It was a tense moment when the Prophet asked:

> 'What mercy can you expect from the man you have persecuted and hounded down for the past twenty years?' asked the Prophet.
> 'We confide in the generosity and kindness of our kinsman,' replied the head Quraysh.
> 'And you shall not confide in vain. Begone! You are safe, you are free,' answered the Prophet.

At this crucial moment, the generosity and magnanimity of the Prophet evidently knew no bounds. He was extremely tender and kindhearted-worthy of earning the title "mercy for mankind." The Quran mentions these noble qualities of the Prophet: *And surely thou [Muhammad] hast sublime morals* (68:4).

The extremely gentle nature of the Prophet was the one of the many winsome qualities of his personality. The Quran mentions this nature as a mercy of God:

> *It is part of the mercy of God that thou dost deal gently with them* (3:159).

> *Now hath come unto you a messenger amongst yourself: It grieves him that ye suffer, ardently anxious is he over you; to the believers is he most kind and merciful* (9:128).

Third Verse:
Master of the Day of Judgment

Though God's mercy, compassion, and forgiveness are strongly emphasized in the verses of the Quran, the Quran also frequently reminds us that He is a "Just Judge." As Esposito states: "God's mercy exists in dialectical tension with His justice."[10]

On that Day of Judgment, God will judge the ethical responsibility and accountability of all individuals. Every human on that Day will simply face his doings, not-doings, and misdoings and accept the judgement upon them. God's justice is based on the premise that God knows and sees all. All individuals are responsible for their deeds and actions. Also, every community will be judged by the standards set forth by their prophets:

> And from each people shall We draw a witness, and We shall say: Produce your proof. Then shall they know that the truth is with God (alone), and the (lies) which they invented will leave them in the lurch (28:75).

> How then if We brought from each people a witness, and We brought thee as a witness against these people (4:41).

Even the prophets themselves will be questioned whether they delivered the message truly to their people:

> *Then shall We question those to whom Our message was sent and those by whom We sent it. And verily We shall recount their whole story with knowledge, for We were never absent (at any time or place)* (7:6-7).

But on that awesome day truth and justice will prevail, and individuals will be responsible for their own acts and deeds; no one will bear another person's burden:

> *Say: 'Ye shall not be questioned as to our sins, nor shall we be questioned as to what ye do'* (34:25).

In the third verse of *surah al-fatihah,* the Arabic word *din* has always been translated as "judgment," which is correct in this context. But the Arabic word *din,* in the Quran, is frequently used for "religion."

> *Today I have perfected your religion for you, and I have completed My blessings upon you, and I have approved for you Islam as a religion* (5:3).

> *Worship God, making thy religion pure for Him. Does not pure religion belong to God* (39:2-3).

> *Judgment belongs only to God. He has commanded that you worship none but Him. that is the right religion, but most people do not know* (12:14).

> *God has laid down for you as religion that which He charged Noah, and what We revealed to thee, and that which We charged Abraham, Moses, and Jesus: 'Perform the religion, and scatter not regarding it'* (42:13).

So why do all expert translators interpret the word *din* as judgment or final judgment in the third verse of the Opening Chapter? The answer becomes clear when we try to understand the root meaning of the word. The root meaning of the word *din* is to obey, to submit, to serve; a closely related word is *dayn* which literally means "debt." It therefore signifies repayment, requital, recompense, reckoning—thus the day of the final judgment in the next world is the day (for payment) of a debt.

The specter of that day, also referred to in the Quran as the "Day of Decision" [*yawm al-fasl*], "Day of Resurrection" [*yawm al-qiyamah*], or "Day of Reckoning" [*yawm al-hisab*], with its eternal reward and punishment, remains a constant reminder of the ultimate consequence of everyone's life. Since God, and God alone, is the Master of the Day of Judgment, He will render justice to all individuals that day. That day, men and women will earn their reward for their acts and deeds in this world: obviously, good deeds and bad deeds cannot have the same reward. The Quran's strong and repeated emphasis on the moral responsibility and accountability of every individual is closely related with the Day of Judgment. The early Meccan chapters contain a very graphic description of the Last Day.

The Quran repeatedly reminds us that on the Day of Judgment, when all of us will return to God, we will give an account of what we have done in this world. The Quran frequently refers to "weighing of deeds" and "giving book or scrolls" in the right hand [to good people] or left hand [to evil people]. On that day, no secret will be hidden, all veils will be lifted, and the deed-records will testify; even a man's thought will become public and his bodily organs will speak for or against him.

> *And (make mention of) the Day when the enemies of God are gathered unto the Fire, they are driven on until, when they reach it, their ears and their eyes and their skins testify against them as to what they used to*

do. And they say unto their skins: Why testify ye against us? They say: God hath given us speech Who giveth speech to all things, and Who created you at the first, and unto Him ye are returned. You did not hide yourself lest your ears and your eyes and your skins should testify against you but ye deemed that God knew not much of what ye did (41:19-22).

According to the Quran, on the Day of Judgment, man will stand before God alone without his friends, relatives or tribes:

You have indeed come to us alone—as alone as we have created you in the first place (6:94; cf. 19:95).

The Quran vividly depicts the state of loneliness without worldly possession and friends. On that awful day even those closest to us in this world will not be willing to help or share each other's sorrow, grief, or humiliation:

When there comes the deafening noise—that day shall a man flee from his own brother, and from his mother, and his father, and from his wife and his children. Each one of them that day, will have enough concern (of his own) to make him indifferent to the others (80:33-37).

When the sky is cleft asunder When the stars are scattered when the oceans are suffered to burst forth; and when the graves are turned upside down, (then) shall each soul know what it hath sent forward; and (what it hath) kept back (82:1-5).

When the earth is shaken to its (utmost) convulsion; and the earth throws up its burdens (from within); and the man cries (distressed) what is the matter with it? On that day will it declare the tidings: for thy Lord will have given its inspiration. On that day will men proceed in

> companies sorted out, to be shown the deeds that they
> (had done). Then shall anyone who has done an atom's
> weight of good, shall see it and anyone who has done
> an atom's weight of evil, shall see it (99:1-8).

That day the human being will be standing alone before God with all veils lifted and no secret hidden. According to the Quran nothing that day will help a person except his good deeds or wholesome deeds. There are constant reminders in the Quran that only true faith and good or wholesome deeds can yield positive results and thus save the individual that day.

> *Whosoever has faith in God and the Last Day and does wholesome deeds—they have their reward with their Lord, and there is no fear upon them, nor shall they grieve* (2:62; cf. 5:69).

> *Give good news to those who have faith and do wholesome deeds that they will have gardens through which rivers flow* (2:25).

> *Whoso does wholesome deed, be it male or female, and has faith, We shall assuredly give him a pleasant life, and We shall recompense them with their wage according to the most beautiful of what they did* (16:97).

> *Those who have faith and do wholesome deeds, them We shall admit to gardens through which rivers flow* (4:57, 4:122).

> *Whoso has faith in God and works wholesome deeds, He shall acquit him of his ugly deeds and cause him to enter the Garden* (64:9).

What are wholesome deeds? The Quranic term *salih*, means "sound, proper, wholesome, good." Quite frequently the Quran uses the terms *salihat* (wholesome deeds) and *salihun* (wholesome people). Two qualities must be present for activities to be wholesome deeds. First, they must be the right activity according to God's commands and teachings of the prophets. Second, those activities must stem from sincere motives [*ikhlas*]. Just to do what God wants you to do is not enough; we must do things for God's sake alone. The Arabic word *ikhlas* means "to purify, to refine, to remove all impurities." Hence its antonyms are *nifaq* [hypocrisy] or *riya* [a false show of something].

Real sincerity is not to make a show for people, but to do things for God's sake, without telling anyone about it. Islamic scholars, Murata and Chittick, beautifully illustrate this point.

> Sincere activity must be done for God's sake alone. Thus, for example, the Koran recommends giving charity to people in addition to the obligatory alms tax. But for this to be true charity, it must be given for God's sake, not for the sake of showing people how generous and pious you are. Moreover, you must never make those to whom you give charity feel indebted to you. After all, it is God who gives them the gift. They should feel indebted to God for everything good. But if you try to make them feel indebted to you, your act is sullied by an ulterior motive.[11]

If we make people feel obliged and hurt them by reminding them of our favors or kindness, we are not doing things for God's sake. The Quran, therefore, issues a stern warning to Muslims against this kind of wrongdoing.

> *A kind word with forgiveness is better than almsgiving followed by injury. God is Absolute and Clement. O ye who believe! do not void your acts of charity by imposing favors and hurting, as does he who spends his wealth to make a show for the people and has no faith in God and the Last Day* (2:263-264).

The final return is to God, and on that Day of Reckoning we will be held accountable: *"Lo! unto Us is their return; and Ours their reckoning"* (88:25-26). The word return is significant. By using the word return, the Quran is reminding us that we will go back, or will be taken back, to the same place we came from. To say people are "returning," means they have been there before.

> *Do you think that We have created you purposelessly and that you will not be returned to us (23:115).*

> *As He originated you, so you will return (7:29).*

> *For to Us will be their return; Then it will be for Us to call them to account (88:25-26).*

> *Does man think that he will be left wandering (at his own whim) (75:36).*

> *We warn you of a doom at hand, a day when man will look on that which his own hands have sent before (78:40).*

> *Every soul is a pledge for its own deeds (74:38).*

> *He created you the first time, and unto Him you shall be taken back (41:21).*

The Quran repeatedly points out that the human being is so absorbed in his selfish, narrow, material concerns that he does not heed the ends of life [al-akhira]. Therefore, the Quran exhorts people, *"to send something for the morrow"* (59:18). Because, *"when the great disaster comes, that day the human being will recall what he had been striving for"* (79:34-35). Still, the human being is more attracted toward the immediate pleasures and is heedless of the long-range goals: *"Nay, but you covet what is immediate and abandon what is distant in time to come"*

(75:20). We keep busy through the tremendous preoccupation with possessions and riches, name and fame, and power and high position. These preoccupations distract us from the "hereafter" and prevent us from preparing and sending forth for the morrow.

> *Nay (behold), ye prefer the life of this world; but the Hereafter is Better and more enduring (87:16-17).*

The Quranic teachings, however, are not against earning wealth. On the contrary, wealth is seen as good, a sign of hard work. It is called "bounty of God"[*fadl Allah*] and "good" [*khair*]. The Quran, however, warns against the dangers of a mad craze for wealth and power that prevents man from pursuing "higher values" and makes him heedless of the Hereafter:

> *Woe to every slanderer, scoffer, who gathers wealth and counts it, thinking wealth will make him immortal. By no means! They shall be flung to destroying flame (104:1-4).*

> *But as for him who hoardeth and deemeth himself independent, and disbelieveth in goodness, surely we will ease his way unto adversity; his riches will not save him when he perisheth. Lo! Ours it is to give the guidance. And verily unto Us (belong) the End and the Beginning (92:8-13).*

At times the Quran directly points out the faults of those who are consumed by their wealth and pride and are heedless of the poor and the needy:

> *Nay, but ye respect not the orphan, urge not to feed the destitute, devour the heritage greedily, love wealth ardently. Nay, but when the earth is ground to atoms, grinding, grinding. And the Lord shall come with angels, rank on rank. And hell is brought near that Day*

man will remember, but how will the remembrance (then avail him) (89:17-23).

Meccan pagans could not accept the idea of resurrection and the Day of Judgment. These ideas were quite foreign to them. They ridiculed the whole idea and did not hesitate to point out that this was no more than an ancient fable:

They say: 'What? when we die and become dust and bones, could we really be raised up again? Such things have been promised to us and to our fathers before; they are nothing but the tale of the ancients' (23: 82-83).

This objection of the Meccan pagans and their tendency to ridicule the Day of Judgment is not much different from the modern person who expresses serious doubts about the Day of Resurrection. When a modern person applies reason to the understanding of these mysteries, they all appear to be fantasy. The mere idea of the next world seems baffling, and it seems totally ridiculous to believe that in the next world a person will suffer the consequences of his bad deeds in this world. But religion is based on faith, an act of emotional commitment, and the religious system is a form of self-transcendence. However, the idea of a next world is not as ridiculous as it may first appear.

An analogy can best illustrate this point. Suppose for a moment that we can somehow talk with the unborn baby in his mother's womb, and that we tell the baby, "Soon you are going to come into a completely different world which is so vast that you cannot even comprehend it. It has mountains, valleys, oceans, trees, fruits, animals, birds, stars, galaxies of which you cannot even conceive." Suppose we also say to the baby, "Do not jump too much in your mother's womb, because if you do, you might damage your brain and suffer all your life in the next world."

How do we think the baby will respond? He will most proba-

36 Essence of the Quran: surah al-fatihah

bly say, "I don't understand what you are talking about. I don't believe in the next world, and it sounds ridiculous that the next world is so vast and different that I can't even comprehend it. And what do you mean by oceans, mountains, animals, birds, and different varieties of fruits? And tell me what do you mean by brain damage, and why and how will I suffer in the next world for what I do here?" Isn't this exactly our situation about the Biblical prophets and the Quranic statements about the Day of Judgment?

The idea of life after death and the final Day of Judgment is one of the basic themes repeated very often in the early passages of the Quran. The Quranic teaching on the Hereafter is that "the Hour" will come when every human will be shaken into an unprecedented self-awareness of his deeds. He will starkly face his own doings and misdoings and accept the judgment upon them. Consequently the Quran continued exhorting people to send something for the morrow, because in the "Hour of Truth" deeds will be weighed and every individual and every community will be judged:

> *On that Day will men proceed in companies sorted out, to be shown the deeds that they (had done) (99:6).*

> *Say our Lord will bring us all together, then He will judge between us with truth; He is the All-Knowing Judge (34:26).*

> *Let those who believe this (Revelation), and those who are Jews, and the Sabaeans and the Christian and the Magians and the idolaters. Lo! God will decide between them on that Day of Resurrection. Lo! God is witness over all things (22:17).*

These Quranic verses clearly identify three basic concepts: every soul, every individual will be held accountable for his acts and deeds and will not be answerable for other people's burdens; there is no concept of "original sin" in Islam; and God and God alone is the Master of the Day of Judgment. The Quran, thus, rejects the three basic Christian doctrines that form the cornerstone of Christian faith.

Since, according to the Quran, no individual will be held responsible for other people's sins and wrongdoing, the Christian belief that Jesus died on the cross for the sins of mankind (Christ's ransom sacrifice for mankind's sin) is not accepted by the Muslims. In fact the Quran never ceases to emphasize that individuals are responsible only for their own acts and deeds and not for others:

> *That was a people that hath passed away. They shall reap the fruit of what they did, and ye of what ye do!. You shall not be asked about what they did* (2:141; cf. 2:134).

> *That we are responsible for our doings and ye for yours* (2:139).

Also the Quran consistently affirms that God alone is the Master of the Day of Judgment; this contradicts the Christian doctrine that Christ, not God, will be the Judge. *"For the Father judgeth no man, but hath committed all judgment unto the Son."* (John 5:23). Again, unlike Christianity, Islam has no notion of an inherited "original sin." The Biblical and Quranic stories about the "fall" reveal the basis for the divergent doctrines of Christianity and Islam.

In the Bible, the "fall" is due to man's flawed nature. The "fall" therefore, brings a life of shame, disgrace, and hardship. According to the Bible, when God asked Adam,

> *'Hast thou eaten of the tree?' Adam responded, 'The woman whom thou gavest to be with me, she gave me of the tree, and I did eat'* (Genesis 3:11-12).

God then addressed to both Adam and Eve:

> *Unto the woman He said, 'I will greatly multiply thy sorrow, and thy conception; in sorrow thou shalt bring forth children; and thy desire shall be thy husband, and he shall rule over thee. And unto Adam He said, 'Because thou hast hearkened unto the voice of thy wife, and hast eaten of the tree of which I commanded thee saying, "Thou shalt not eat of it," cursed is the ground for thy sake; in sorrow shalt thou eat of it all the days of life. Thorns and thistles shall it bring forth for thee; and thou shalt eat the herb of the field'* (Genesis 3:16-18).

The Biblical account is not as devastating as it later became when Christian theologians attempted to expound the concept of "original sin." They highly denigrated sexuality and put all the blame on women. Tertullian's statement about women is certainly grotesque:

> Do you know that you are each an Eve? The sentence of God on this sex of yours lives in this age: the guilt must of necessity live too. You are the devil's gateway; you are the unsealer of that forbidden tree; you are first deserter of the divine law. . . . you so carelessly destroyed man, God's image. On account of your desert, even the Son of God had to die.[12]

Unfortunately, St. Augustine further endorsed this deranged thinking. In a letter to his friend he wrote, "What is the difference whether it is in a wife or a mother, it is still Eve the temptress that we must beware of in any woman." (On the Trinity, xiii)

Though the Quran does not mention the creation of Eve, it tells us that God placed both of them in the garden and gave specific instructions:

> *And We said: Adam, dwell you, and your wife, in the garden and eat ye freely wherever you desire; but do*

> *not come near this tree, lest you be wrongdoers. But Satan caused them to slip therefrom and brought them out of what they were in* (2:35-36).

Since, according to the Quran, the devil did not solely tempt Eve, a woman is not portrayed as the "temptress" as it is done in the Judeo-Christian traditions. Further the sin of Adam and Eve is considered their personal sin. This sin was an act of disobedience for which they alone were responsible. It was not a sin committed by the human race for which all humanity must suffer. The Quran taught that after disobeying God, Adam repented and asked His forgiveness and guidance: *"But his Lord chose him. He turned to him and gave him guidance"* (22:122).

Also, the story of Adam and Iblis [Satan] in the Quran has a strong moral tone. Despite God's clear order, Iblis for the first time decided to disobey. And when God asked Iblis, *"What prevented you from prostrating yourself to him [Adam],"* he replied, *"I am better than he. You created me of fire, but You created him of clay"* (7:12, 38:75-76). After that we all know the story—God sent Iblis out of heaven in disgrace, and since then he has been busy trying to seduce and beguile the children of Adam.

One thing that clearly emerges from the story of Iblis is his self-assertive arrogance, as if he is saying "I am made of fire, I am better than he. I will do my own thing, and ignore God's command." This attitude of arrogance reflecting haughty and insolent behavior is called *"istikbar"* in Quranic language. The Quran gives repeated warnings that God does not love those who are boastful, arrogant, and vainglorious:

> *So enter the gates of Hell, to dwell therein. Thus evil indeed is the abode of the arrogant* (16:29).

> *And swell not thy cheek (for pride) at men. Nor walk in insolence through the earth: For God loveth not any arrogant boaster* (31:18).

> *For God loveth not the arrogant, the vainglorious* (4:36).

> *Nor walk on the earth with insolence: for thou canst not rend the earth asunder, nor reach the mountains in height. The evil of all that is hateful in the sight of thy Lord* (17:37-38).

While God condemns haughtiness and arrogance, He also reminds people not to despair and become oblivious to God's mercy. In fact, helplessness and utter despair is the result of losing the anchorage point with God—the Everlasting Refuge. The state of desperation is, therefore, described as a hallmark of "unbelievers."

> *Lo! None despaireth of the Spirit of God save disbelieving folk* (12:87).

> *Despair not of the mercy of God, Who forgiveth all sins. Lo! He is Oft-Forgiving, the Merciful* (39:53).

Fourth Verse:
Thee (Alone) We Worship, Thee (Alone) We Ask For Help

This verse categorically states that the human being must worship God and God alone and only seek His help. This ends once and for all every type of polytheism [shirk] whether manifest or hidden. God alone is worthy of being worshiped and He alone is the Protector, Sustainer, and Cherisher of the worlds. Therefore, we must turn to God and God alone for His help, mercy, and forgiveness.

Consequently, Islam has no priesthood, no intermediary, and no intercessor. There is direct relationship between God and the human being. According to the Quranic teachings every individual must directly turn to God, Whose everlasting mercy extends to all creatures:

> *And saith your Lord: call on me and I will answer your (prayer)* (40:60).

> *Is not He who listens to the distressed when he crieth unto Him and relieves the suffering* (27:62).

> *Wherever ye turn, there is the face of God* (2:115).

> *God cometh in between man and his own heart* (8:24).

> We (God) are nearer to him (man) than his jugular vein (50:16).

> As for those who strive in Us, We surely guide them to Our paths (29:69).

The Quran vehemently denounces any form of polytheism. According to the Quran, this is the fundamental error at the root of all sin and transgression. In Quranic lexicon the word *"shirk"* implies—"assigning partners to God, or worshiping someone along with God, or allowing anything to usurp God's place." This word is used in nearly seventy-five verses of the Quran.

Actually, *shirk* is the fundamental state of being in revolt against God, any professed belief in other gods. *Shirk* is also atheism or the putting of nothingness in the place of God. *Shirk* is the opposite of surrender to God [*islam*], which is acceptance and recognition of His Reality. Indeed *shirk* is considered an unforgivable sin:

> God forgiveth not (the sin of) joining other gods with Him; but He forgiveth whom He pleaseth other sins than this: one who joins other gods with God, hath strayed far, far away (from the right) (4:116).

> Whoso ascribeth partners to God, has indeed forged a mighty sin (4:48).

The monotheism of Islam is preserved in the doctrine of the Unity, Oneness [*tawhid*]. The Unity of God is the central theme of Islam. Indeed, "this Unity" is the basis of salvation. The concept of *tawhid* is usually explained and understood in two ways: all-exclusive and all-inclusive. The all-exclusive approach is based upon the negation [*nafy*] as revealed in the the testimony of faith [*shahadah*]—there is no god but God. This emphasizes the exclusive aspect; utter exclusion of any analogy and similarity in creation that reflects God's attributes. The all-inclusive approach means that "nothing is outside God." This approach attracted most Sufis. For the Sufis, the realization of the oneness of God [*tawhid*] is union with God. One must hasten to point out that Sufis were extremely cautious and clearly stated that the unification with God does not mean that the difference between God and the servant disappears. They insisted that the Lord remains the Lord, and the servant remains the servant.

The famous Sufi (Muslim mystic) and philosopher ibn al-Arabi (d. 1240 AD) presented his scholarly work on this subject in his two books: *Risalat al-ahadiyyah* [Treatise on Oneness] and *Wahdat al wujud* [The Unity of Being]. The traditional, all-exclusive viewpoint is best preserved in the writings of Ibn Abd al-Wahhab (d. 1787 AD).

Whether one accepts the traditional approach, the Sufi approach, or an eclectic approach, there is no dispute on the issue that God's will or law is comprehensive and it extends to all creatures and all domains of life. Consequently, no prophet, no saint, no Sufi mystic will ever be given a status which in any way reflects that we are, even figuratively speaking, seeking their help or protection.

The Quran severely censures the Jews and Christians for treating priests and rabbis with such high veneration that their decisions and verdicts attained finality as if they were revealed by God:

> *They take their priests and their rabbis to be their lords in derogation of God* (9:31).

According to an authentic tradition (*hadith*), Adi ibn Hatim [who converted from Christianity to Islam] once asked the Prophet to clarify a few questions that had been troubling him. One of the questions that he asked for clarification was about this revelation (9:31). Adi ibn Hatim stated that since Christians did not treat their priests as God, how would we explain this revelation? The Prophet remarked that Christian and Jews held their priests and rabbis in such a high degree of adoration that their verdicts became law; their statements about lawful [*halal*] and unlawful [*haram*] ultimately attained the same status as if they were the commands of God. When Adi ibn Hatim agreed, the Prophet stressed the point that the elevation of human beings to the status of a quasi-divine law-giver is no different than treating them as God.

It is time for Muslims to pause and reflect on the meaning and significance of this Quranic verse. Very often we summarily dismiss the whole issue by simply stating that this ritual or doctrine is according to our Imam, or according to our Hanafi School [or Shafi'i, Malaki, or Hanbali as the case may be], and rigidly adhere to our viewpoint. In his commentary on this verse, **Maulana Abu 'l-Ala Mawdudi (d. 1979 AD)** remarked:

> It is, therefore, clear that without the evidentiary support of God's book [Quran] those who set the guideline and make things lawful or unlawful and impose them on mankind are actually appointing themselves as God; and those who grant these rights to those human beings to impose these guidelines are treating them as God.[13]

Sadly, rules and regulations which now govern the behavior of so many Muslims are derived from the lego-religious books with which the Islamic world is flooded. Lamenting this present condition, the Indian scholar Syed Ameer Ali stated:

> The lives and conduct of a large number of Moslems (*sic*) at the present day are governed less by the precepts and teachings of the Master (the Prophet), and more by the theories and opinions of the *mujtahids* and *imams* who have tried, each according to his light, to construe the revelations vouchsafed to the Teacher. Like men in a crowd listening to a preacher who from a lofty position addresses a large multitude and from

his vantage ground overlooks a vast area, they observed only their immediate surroundings, and, without comprehending the wider meaning of his words or the nature of the audience whom he addressed, adapted his utterances to their own limited notions of human needs and human progress. Oblivious of the universality of the Master's teachings, unassisted by his spirit, devoid of his inspiration, they forgot that the Prophet, from the pinnacle of his genius, has spoken to all humanity. They mixed up the temporary with the permanent, the universal with the particular.[14]

In all ages, people have succumbed to the superstition of priest worship and saint worship. Many Islamic scholars have paid special attention to the various types of assigning partners to God [*shirk*] that may not be as crude as worshiping man-made idols. The famous Shah Wali Allah (d. 1762 AD) and the renowned ibn Abd al Wahhab (d. 1787 AD) have seriously warned Muslims against many hidden or latent types of *shirk* of which we may not be fully cognizant. These Muslim scholars have pointed out three main types of polytheism [*shirk*]: ascribing knowledge of hidden things [*shirk al-ilm*] to others than God [*alam al-ghaib*]; ascribing power to others than God or supposing that anyone has power with God [*shirk al-tasarruf*]; worshiping anyone other than God [*shirk al-ibadah*] or all such practices which are associated with offering worship to created things.

The Companions of the Prophet, especially those who were closest to him, knew this weakness of human beings too well and some of their early decisions reflected their sensitivity to this issue. When the whole Muslim community was suddenly shaken by the death of the Prophet, the speech of Abu Bakr gave the sobering warning:

> O people, whoso hath been wont to worship Muhammad—verily Muhammad is dead; and whoso

46 Essence of the Quran: surah al-fatihah

wont to worship God, verily God is living and dieth not.

Then he recited the following verse of the Quran:

> *Muhammad is no more than a messenger; many messengers have passed away before him. If he die or be slain, will ye then turn upon your heels? Whoso turneth upon his heels will thereby do no hurt unto God; and God will reward the thankful* (3:144).

Extremely high veneration of religious leaders—whether they be rabbis, priests, ministers, or religious scholars [*ulama*]—reflect superstitions centered on priest-worship, especially when carried to the point of total submission or infallibility. This is a kind of polytheism [*shirk*]. Therefore, according to the Quranic teachings the mere idea of a separate order of priesthood to stand between God and the human being is a malediction. Syed Ameer Ali explains this point.

> The Islam of Mohammed recognizes no caste of priesthood, allows no monopoly of spiritual knowledge or special holiness to intervene between man and his God. Each soul rises to its Creator without the intervention of priest or hierophant. No sacrifice, no ceremonial, invented by vested interests, is needed to bring the anxious heart nearer to his Comforter. Each human being is his own priest; in the Islam of Mohammed no one man is higher than the other.[15]

The Quran clearly states that God is nearer to man than his jugular vein (50:16). No matter when and where we seek His help, He is there: *"To God belong the East and the West: wherever ye turn, there is the face of God"* (2:115).

The teachings of the Quran are clear. God is our only Helper, He is *"al-Samad"* the Everlasting Refuge. By accepting God as the only Helper, one is free from all types of polytheism [*shirk*] including the worship of people who sometimes because of their immense wealth, power, and influence behave as gods.

> The likeness of those who choose other patrons than God is as the likeness of the spider when she taketh unto herself a house, and lo! the frailest of all houses is the spider's house, if they but knew (29:41).

There is one other important dimension of assigning partners to God [*shirk*] that has been grossly underemphasized. It is therefore necessary to clarify this aspect fully. It is true *shirk* implies worshiping anyone except God, but to follow one's own desire or caprice is also a form of *shirk*, and very often it is concealed or camouflaged by those who appear outwardly pious.

> Hast thou seen him who maketh his desire his god, and God sendeth him astray purposely, and sealeth up his hearing and his heart, and setteth on his sight a covering (45:23).

Worshiping idols in the crude and literal sense of the term is clear and plain and, therefore, easier to deal with. But the habit of worshiping one's own desire or caprice as god is deceptive and dangerous. The Prophet, therefore was more concerned about this hidden and deceptive type of *shirk* than the obvious idolatry or paganism. The following *hadith* illustrates this point very well:

> The Prophet came out to us from his house while we were discussing the Antichrist. He said, 'Shall I tell you something that is more frightening than the Antichrist?' The people replied that he should. He said, 'Hidden *shirk*. In other words, that a man should perform the salah and do it beautifully for the sake of someone who is watching.'

In another *hadith* the Prophet makes it distinctly clear why he was so much distressed that his Community [*ummah*] may fall prey to this hidden *shirk*:

> The most frightening thing that I fear for my *ummah* is associating others with God. I do not mean to say they will worship the sun, or the moon, or idols. I mean they will perform work for other than God with a hidden desire.

FIFTH VERSE:
SHOW US THE STRAIGHT PATH

A right path or straight path implies a path that leads mankind to piety and righteousness—closer to God's grace and mercy. First we are asking God to show, lead, and guide us to the straight path because without His guidance we may wander or drift aimlessly in the darkness. This guidance [*hidaya*] comes from God, Who, through His prophets has revealed His message and has shown man "the Way." Therefore, the Quran calls itself guidance for mankind [*huda li-nas*]. The Quran never claimed to be the only guidance. On the contrary, the Quran teaches that this guidance has always been available to mankind of all ages:

> *He hath ordained for you that religion which He commanded unto Noah, and that which He commanded unto Abraham, Moses and Jesus, saying: establish the religion, and be not divided therein. Dreadful for the idolaters is that unto which thou callest them. God chooseth for Himself whom He will, and guideth unto Himself him who turneth (towards Him) (42:13).*
>
> *And when Abraham said to his father and his folk: Lo I am innocent of what ye worship. Save Him Who did create me, for He will guide me (43:26-27).*
>
> *And as for Thamud, We gave them guidance, but*

> they preferred blindness to guidance, so bolt of the doom of humiliation overtook them because of what they used to earn (41:17).
>
> Lo! Ours it is to (give) the guidance. And lo! unto Us belong the latter portion and the former (92:12-13).
>
> And for those who strive in Us, We surely guide them to Our paths, and lo! God is with the good (29:69).

True guidance is divine guidance. This point is very important and needs to be explained further. That religion provides anchorage point and gives meaning and purpose to life, is clearly explained by Jesus when he gives the example of a person who built:

> an house, and digged deep, and laid the foundation on a rock; and when the flood arose, the storm beat vehemently upon the house and could not shake it; for it was founded upon a rock (Luke 6:48).

In the same way, religion is like a firm rock, and the storm and stress of everyday life do not make us falter; we do not become unsteady, or vacillate, or fall victim to malignant doubts and fears. Few can deny the consoling power, the healing strength, and the comforting balm of religion. In fact, religion helps us discover how to reconcile ourselves to the formidable facts of life and death.

For many decades modern medicine and especially psychiatry treated religion as a vestige of pre-scientific era. But this attitude is now changing. A growing body of scientific evidence suggests that religion may have immense healing power; in fact, it may have a direct impact on the body's immunological defenses against disease. Thus the salutary effect of religion isn't limited to mental health; it has a positive impact on physical health. Recently the researchers found lower rates of depression and anxiety-related illness among the religiously committed.[16, 17, 18] As TIME magazine recently reported:

> A 1995 study at Dartmouth-Hitchcock Medical Center found that one of the best predictors of survival among 232 heart-surgery patients was the degree to which the patients said they drew comfort and strength from religious faith. Those who did not had more than three times the death rate of those who did. . . .
>
> A study conducted by National Institute on Aging (1996) revealed that people who regularly attended religious services have been found to have lower blood pressure, less heart disease, lower rates of depression and generally better health than those who don't attend.[19]

All the higher religions of the world demand from the human being, as a social being, certain behavior in his relationships with his fellows: we call these demands a code of moral conduct. In fact, religion and morality are interdependent; the concept of good and bad, or any consistent value system, can hardly exist independently of religion. The higher religions have generated all the codes of moral conduct that have formulated the character of human beings and have given birth to the civilized world. The noble teachings of Buddha, the invaluable Ten Commandments of Moses, the unsurpassed self-sacrificing spirit of Jesus, Muhammad's unparalleled example of universal brotherhood—all these examples have formed the backbone of moral conduct in the civilized parts of the world.

All higher religions tend to emphasize that the individual is not someone in his own right but a part of many inter-dependent cycles, and he is charged with more involvement than just the fulfilment of his own selfish desires. The Ten Commandments revealed to Moses on Mount Sinai (Exodus XX) emphasize the need to establish a viable social order. Similarly, the Twelve Commandments, revealed to the Prophet Muhammad during his mystical ascension to heaven [*al-miraj*] constitute a comprehensive code of moral conduct. Two eminent Muslim scholars, Maulana Syed Sulaiman Nadvi[20] and Hamidullah[21] have distinctly identified the following twelve commandments as mentioned in *surah al-isra* (17:23-38):

> 1. Thy Lord hath decreed that ye worship none but Him.
> 2. And ye be kind to parents . . . and address them in terms of honor, and out of kindness lower to them the wing of humility.
> 3. And give the kinsmen their due rights, and the needy and wayfarer.
> 4. Squander not thy wealth in wantonness and keep not thy hand (like a miser) chained to thy neck.
> 5. Kill not your children for fear of want.
> 6. Nor come nigh to adultery; for it is a shameful (deed).
> 7. Do not take the life which God hath forbidden save with right.
> 8. And do not touch the sustenance of an orphan, save to improve it.
> 9. And fulfill the covenant; verily [on Judgement Day] you will be called to account for every covenant.
> 10. And give full measure when you measure and weigh with a straight balance.
> 11. And pursue not that of which thou hast no knowledge.
> 12. And walk not on the earth with insolence. . . . it is hateful in the sight of thy Lord.

During the past four decades, the process of secularization has been carried to the extreme in the West. The moral and religious values have been gradually demolished and they are being replaced by the "new morality" or "situation ethics." Since, in the modern world the new morality is embedded in situation ethics, there is an unrealistic expectation that the behavioral scientists will soon reveal the real truth on which we can erect the edifice of a new morality. Since nothing can be further from the truth, it is time to explode this myth.

The so-called experts of behavioral science have gradually usurped the field of moral and social values. There is a new trend, especially among modern youth, to see morality and ethical codes as independent of religion. They believe that in this modern world behavioral scientists are the experts, and they should lay down the foundation of a new morality based on truth and facts discovered through painstaking research in the various disciplines of behavioral science. The story of Nasruddin, as it has been told and retold by the Sufis, keeps coming to my mind as I contemplate the expectation of modern youth to find real truth from the behavioral scientists:

One night Nasruddin's friends observed him crawling around on his hands and knees anxiously searching for something beneath a lamp post. When they asked him what he was looking for, he told them that he had lost the key to his house. All his friends got down to help him look, but no one could find the key. Feeling frustrated one of them asked Nasruddin where exactly he had lost the key. Nasruddin responded, "In the house." Then why," his friends questioned, " are you looking under the lamp-post?" Nasruddin replied, "Because there is light here."

Behavioral scientists have certainly formulated many hypotheses and theories to explain some issues concerning human behavior, yet searching for real truth in the field of behavioral science is like Nasruddin searching for his key in the wrong place.

However, this "scientific myth" or "scientific superstition" runs deep and is difficult to eradicate because behavioral scientists and most clinicians, while claiming to be scientific in their approach, usually adopt the role of moral arbiters. There is no such thing as basic truth or fundamental law in the field of behavioral science. Human behavior is so unpredictable, affected

54 Essence of the Quran: surah al-fatihah

by so many factors within and around the individual and subject to so many unforeseen turns of fortune, that a change in behavior can rarely be ascribed to any particular factor unless there is clear and compelling evidence.

The scientific outlook of the behaviorist is sheer fantasy simply because there are few relevant aspects of human behavior which lend themselves to quantitative measurement. Those who try to cling to the mechanistic model of human behavior have produced a purely jaundiced view of the human being, denying those faculties which are not found in lower animals. This has been rightly called the "ratamorphic" view of man.[22]

Though we now have a massive amount of literature bearing on the various aspects of human behavior, students of this field have erected a latter day Babel. The confusion and vagueness are so overwhelming that on practically any important issue, depending on the initial bias of the investigator, scientific data have been used to support diametrically opposite points of view.

So behavioral scientists have little to offer. True guidance is only divine guidance from God. We are, therefore, earnestly asking Him to show us the straight path [*sirat al-mustaqim*], but we are also asking His guidance to help us to remain on the path of righteousness. Just finding the right path is not enough; we also need His guidance to remain steadfast on the path of righteousness. However, the Quran makes it explicitly clear that righteousness does not mean strict observance of certain religious ritual or practices; it must lead to God's consciousness, called *"taqwa"* in the Quran.

Taqwa, in fact, is the central theme that runs throughout the Quran; and it is the basic or fundamental teaching of the Prophet Muhammad. Very often, external forms or trappings of the religion are overemphasized, but they do not correspond to its innermost spiritual element. According to the Indian Muslim scholar, Syed Sulaiman Nadvi, "If one has to describe in one word the central theme of the teachings of the Prophet Muhammad, it can be expressed by the word *taqwa*."[23] Fazlur Rahman, an erudite scholar of the Quran, also stated that, "The term *taqwa* is perhaps the most important single term in the Quran. . . . The central endeavor of the Quran is for man to develop this keen insight (*taqwa*)."[24]

The word "*taqwa*" comes from the root word "*wqy*" which means "to guard or protect against." This would imply that one can protect oneself by always keeping God in view because God sees not only our actions but also our thoughts.

> *If you do what is good and are God-wary—surely God is aware of what you do* (4:128).
>
> *Be wary of God, and know that God sees what you do* (2:233).
>
> *Be wary of God. Surely God knows the thoughts in the breasts* (5:7).
>
> *Be wary of God, and know that you will be mustered to Him* (2:203).

Taqwa, as a central theme of the Islamic teaching, is consistently mentioned in the Quran. According to the Quran, it should be the primary motivating force behind all our endeavors; without achieving *taqwa*, our efforts are meaningless.

> *It is not righteousness that ye turn your faces to the East and the West; but righteousness is he who believeth in God and the Last Day and the angels and the scripture and the Prophets; and giveth his wealth, for love of Him, to kinsfolk and to orphans and the needy and the wayfarer, and to those ask, and to set slaves free; and observeth proper worship and payeth the poor due. And those who keep the treaty when they made one, and the patient in tribulation and adversity and time of stress. Such are those who are sincere. Such are the God-fearing* (2:177).

Here, a number of qualities have been identified for those who are successful in achieving God-wariness [*taqwa*, righteousness]. For protecting our soul against temptations of evils and wrongdoings, we must have complete faith and trust in God. There are variations in the English translation of the word *taqwa* by scholars. It has been translated as: God-fearing, ward off or guard against evil, piety, righteousness, God's consciousness, and God-wariness. In fact, all these translations are equally correct because the word *taqwa* is quite comprehensive and it has been used in many different contexts in the Quran. *Taqwa*, in the strict Quranic sense, "is a kind of inner light, torch, or a spiritual spark which a man must light within himself. Without this he will fail to distinguish between right or wrong, truth and falsehood, seeming and real, immediate and lasting."[25] The first verse of the second chapter of the Quran confirms that this book is a guidance only for those who possess *taqwa* [*muttaqi*].

> This is a Scripture wherein there is no doubt, a guidance unto those who ward off (evil) (2:1).

The purpose of all our worship [*ibadah*] is to attain *taqwa*:

> O mankind! Worship your Lord, Who hath created you and those before you, so that ye may ward off (evil) (2:21).

Also the main purpose of keeping fast is to attain *taqwa*:

> O ye who believe! Fasting is prescribed for you, even as it was prescribed for those before you, that ye may ward off (evil) (2:183).

And when we perform the pilgrimage (*hajj*) and hold in honor the symbols of God, these activities should come from the heart of *taqwa*:

> *Such (in his state): and Whoever holds in honor the symbols of God, (in the sacrifice of animals), Such (honor) should come truly from the piety of heart (22:32).*

Similarly, during the pilgrimage when we revitalize the memory of Abraham and sacrifice animals, the main goal is *taqwa*:

> *It is not their meat, nor their blood, that reaches God; it is piety that reaches Him (22:37).*

While the Quran recommends that we take a provision for the journey, it stresses that the best provision is *taqwa*:

> *And take a provision (with you) for the journey, but the best of provisions is right conduct, so keep your duty unto Me, O men of understanding (2:197).*

When we are advised to cover our body with garments, the Quran again emphasizes that *taqwa* is the best garment:

> *O ye children of Adam! We have bestowed raiment upon you to cover your shame, as well as adornment to you. But the raiment of righteousness that is the best (7:26).*

Forgiving others brings us closer to *taqwa*:

> *To forgo is nearer to piety, and forget not kindness among yourselves. God is Seer of what ye do (2:237).*

When we are trying to remain just and fair to our enemies, we are at the threshold of *taqwa*:

> *O ye believe! Stand out firmly for God, as witnesses to fair dealing, and let not the hatred of others to*

> you make you swerve to wrong and depart from justice. Be just: this is next to piety (5:8).

Again on the question of doing justice and giving true testimony, the commands of the Quran are very explicit.

> O you who believe! Establish justice, being witness for God,-even if the evidence goes against yourselves or against your parents or kinsmen; and irrespective of whether the witness is rich or poor, under all circumstances God has priority for you [over your relatives] (4:135).

Islam also obliterated all distinctions among men on the basis of race, color, and national origin. The Quran confirmed that the essence of all human rights is the equality of all of the human races:

> The noblest of you in the sight of God is the one most possessed of taqwa (49:13).

Taqwa is a shield in the conscience of the individual which can be used as a defense against temptations to do evil deeds leading to inequity and moral degradation. In the Quranic context taqwa also represents social dimensions. Purification of one's soul, heart, or conscience is not enough; one must assume responsibility for the prevention of evils in society; whether it is moral degradation, persecution, oppression, or social injustice. The Quran keeps reminding Muslims "to command good and forbid evil." The new Muslim community was described in the Quran as:

> Ye are the best community that has been raised up for mankind. Ye command good and forbid evil; and ye believe in God (3:110).

It is fair to assume that according to the devotion and sincerity of faith, *taqwa* of an individual is capable of gradations. Those who attained the highest stages of *taqwa*, completely surrender to God and their efforts and endeavors are totally directed to serve God and God alone:

> *Say: Lo! my worship and my sacrifice and my living and my dying are for God, Lord of the worlds* (6:162).

SIXTH VERSE:
THE PATH OF THOSE
WHOM THOU HAST FAVORED

After asking God to guide us to the straight path, it is now further requested that He show us the straight path of all those people whom He has favored. Again, it is emphasized that true religion was revealed to many nations throughout the world and it was not confined to a particular nation or tribe. Since no nation or tribe has a monopoly on God's true religion, there were righteous and God fearing people in every nation and every age. As Armstrong explains:

> Because there was only one God, all rightly guided religions must derive from Him alone. Belief in the supreme and sole Reality would be culturally conditioned and would be expressed by different societies in different ways, but the focus of all true worship must have been inspired by and directed toward the being whom the Arabs had always called al-Lah.[26]

Followers of other faiths never fully realized this important point that God sent His messengers in every age and the Prophet Muhammad never claimed to have brought a new message. Consequently, it had caused a number of misunderstandings. There are two main reasons why this happened. When the tide of

Islam rapidly rolled eastward and westward and many nations in many different countries embraced Islam, it automatically sparked a fire of jealousy, bordering upon hostility among other faiths. Due to this negative environment people ignored even simple basic teachings of the Prophet. Also when the Muslim empire was at its zenith, the imperialistic attitude of the Muslims may have fostered this kind of thinking. When intellectually challenged by religious leaders of other faiths, Muslims, in their zeal to defend the faith of Islam, at times adopted a non-conciliatory attitude toward other faiths.

However, contrary to the Biblical accounts, God did not reveal this true religion [*islam*] only to one tribe, because He had a special liking for a particular nation or people. It is repeatedly mentioned in the Quran that God, Who is Lord of the worlds and all mankind, has revealed this true religion [islam] through His messengers in all ages to all nations.

> *And there is no nation wherein a warner has not come* (35:24).

> *For every people a guide(messenger) has been provided* (13:7).

While some prophets are mentioned, not all prophets are identified in the Quran.

> *And messengers We have mentioned unto thee before and messengers We have not mentioned unto thee* (4:164).

Unfortunately even now Western people have been slow to recognize that it is the basic teaching of the Quran that God's guidance had already been revealed to Jews and Christians. Karen Armstrong, therefore, felt a need to emphasize this point:

> Muhammad never asked Jews and Christians to convert to his religion of al-Lah unless they particularly wished to do so, because they had received authentic revelations of their own. The Koran did not see revelation as canceling out the messages and insights of previous prophets, but instead it stressed the continuity of the religious experience of mankind. It is important to stress this point because tolerance is not a virtue that many Western people today would feel inclined to attribute to Islam. Yet from the start, Muslims saw revelations in less exclusive terms than either Jews or Christians. The intolerance that many people condemn in Islam today does not always spring from a rival vision of God but from quite another source: Muslims are intolerant of injustice, whether this is committed by rulers of their own—like Shah Muhammad Reza Pahalvi of Iran-or by the powerful Western countries. The Koran does not condemn other religious traditions as false or incomplete but shows each new prophet as confirming and continuing the insights of his predecessors.[27]

Since the message revealed to the Prophet Muhammad is not new, the Quran asked that Muslims recognize their bond to older religions.

> *And argue not with the people of the Scripture unless it be in the most kindly manner; unless it be such of them as set on evil doing-and say: we believe in that which hath been revealed unto us and revealed unto you; our God and your God is One, and unto Him we [all] surrender ourselves* (29:46-47).

Muslims were also told that they must show equal respect to all the Prophets and not to arbitrarily make distinctions:

> Say (O Muslims): We believe in God and that which is revealed unto us and that which was revealed unto Abraham and Ishmael, and Isaac, and Jacob, and the tribes, and that which Moses and Jesus received, and that which the Prophets received from their Lord. We make no distinction between any of them, and unto Him we have surrendered (2:136).

All religious bigotry, intolerance, and fanaticism are condemned in Islam. The right of the people to worship God and follow the divine law as revealed to them should never be tampered with. The Glorious Quran categorically states: *"There is no compulsion in religion"* (2:256); and *"Unto you your religion and unto me my religion"* (109:6). The Prophet set an excellent example by allowing Christian from Najran to worship in the sacred mosque of Medina.

Since such an illustrious example of tolerance and generosity is seldom practiced these days, let us quote the leading Muslim scholar Martin Lings,

> Deputations still continued to come as in the previous year, and one of these was from the Christians of Najran, who sought to make a pact with the Prophet. They were of the Byzantine rite, and in the past had received rich subsidies from Constantinople. The delegates, sixty in number, were received by the Prophet in the Mosque, and when the time for their prayer came he allowed them to pray it there, which they did, facing towards the east.[28]

All prophets recognized the "One universal God," but the divine message about laws was different because they were culturally conditioned. The Quran stresses this point, *"For each we have appointed a divine law and a traced-out way"* (5:48). Therefore each community will be judged according to the message it received. Why? Because God wanted it so. The Quran is quite emphatic on this point:

> *Had God willed He would have made you one people. But He hath made you as ye are that he may put you to the test in what he hath given you. So vie with one another in good works. Unto God ye will be brought back and He will then tell you about those things wherein ye differed* (5:48).

Ibn al-Arabi, one of the greatest philosophers and Sufis of his time [d. 1240 AD], attempted to explain this message of the Quran:

> Do not attach yourself to any particular creed exclusively, so that you may disbelieve all the rest; otherwise you will lose much good, nay, you will fail to recognize the real truth of the matter. God, the Omnipresent and Omnipotent, is not limited by any one creed, for he says, *'Wheresoever ye turn, there is the face of God.'*

All Sufis consistently stressed the fact that various religious forms were cultural derivations of the same basic *din*. Ibn al-Arabi illustrates this point eloquently:

> My heart has opened unto every form: The heart varies in accordance with variations of the innermost consciousness. It may appear in the form of a gazelle meadow, a monkish cloister, an idol-temple, a pilgrim kaba, the tablets of the Torah for certain sciences, the bequest of the leaves of the Quran. I practice the religion of Love; in whatsoever directions its caravans advance, the religion of Love shall be my religion and my faith.[29]

The Quran, with which the wheel of revelation has come a full circle, makes a special point that all mankind must be brought back to the original truth, Islam, as taught by Abraham.

> And who forsaketh the religion of Abraham save him who befooleth himself? Verily we chose him in the world, and lo! in the Hereafter he is among the righteous. When his Lord said unto him: Surrender! [aslam] he said: I have surrendered to the Lord of the worlds. The same did Abraham enjoin upon his sons, and also Jacob (saying): O my son! Lo Allah hath chosen for you (true) religion; therefore die not save as men who have surrendered (unto Him). Or were ye present when death came to Jacob, when he said unto his sons: What will ye worship after me? They said: We will worship thy God, the God of Abraham, Ishmael and Isaac, one God and unto Him we all surrender (2:130-133).

All the prophets, especially the Biblical prophets, preached *islam*, the universal religion.

> Say (O Muslims): We believe in God and that which is revealed unto us and that which was revealed unto Abraham and Ishmael, a and Isaac and Jacob, and the tribes, and that which Moses and Jesus received, and the which the Prophets received from their Lord. We make no distinction between any one of them, and unto Him we have surrendered (2:136).

Islam is God's eternal religion described in the Quran as " the primordial nature upon which God created mankind" (30:30). The root *"slm"* in Arabic means, " to be in peace, to be an integral whole." From this root comes *"islam"* meaning to "surrender to God's law and thus to be an integral whole," and Muslim is a person "who surrenders." Two other key terms used in the Quran with high frequency have similar root meanings: *iman*, from the word *"aman"* which means, " to be safe or at peace with oneself," and *taqwa*, from the word *"wqy"* which means "to protect or save." In this context, and in a much wider sense, the Quran declares that *"islam"* is the only true religion:

> *Behold, the only [true] religion before God is islam [man's surrender or submission unto Him]* (3:19).

In this sense the Quran describes Abraham, Isaac, Ishmael, Moses, and Jesus as "Muslims [those who have surrendered]." Unfortunately, certain terms of the Quran, especially the word *"islam,"* became so highly institutionalized during the period of Muslim history, that the original meaning was lost. But to understand the Quran and its message accurately, we must keep in mind the original meaning of the word when the Quran was revealed at the time of the Prophet. This point was fully recognized by the famous Western scholar Muhammad Asad.[30] Unfortunately Muslims and non-Muslims both have failed to realize that the word *"islam"* has been used in the Quran in a "generic" sense. When the Prophet and his Companions used the term *"islam,"* they understood it to denote "man's self-surrender to God," and similarly the term *"muslim"* meant "one who surrenders to God." They never limited these terms to any specific community or denomination.

It, therefore, made perfect sense to the Companions of the Prophet when the Quran spoke of Abraham as one who has *"surrendered himself to God [musliman]"* (3:67); or where the disciples of Jesus state, *"Bear thou witness that we have surrendered ourselves unto God [muslimum]"* (3:52). Consequently, the Noble Quran states that the Muslims believe the revelations received by Jews and Christians because they believe in the same God:

> *We believe in the Revelation which has come down to us and in that which came down to you; our God and your God is one, and it is to Him we surrender [muslimun]* (29:46).

But, unfortunately, later Muslims used the word *"islam"* in a purely restricted sense: they applied it exclusively to the followers of the Prophet Muhammad. The Quran, however, made it clear that God does not favor any individual or nation. Whoever has faith in God and the Last Day and does wholesome deeds will be rewarded by the Lord. Repudiating the claims of Jews and Christians that they alone will enter paradise, the Quran states that God will save anyone who believes in God and the Last Day and does good deeds.

> *And they say: None entereth Paradise unless he be a Jew or Christian. These are their own desire. Say: Bring your proof (of what ye state) if ye are truthful. Nay, but whosoever surrenders himself to God while he does good deeds as well, he shall find his reward with his Lord; and there shall no fear come upon them neither shall they grieve (2:111-112).*

The Quran gives a stern warning to the Muslims—that they are not indispensable and they will be replaced if they do not honestly follow genuine Islamic teachings:

> *O you who have faith, should any of you turn back on your religion, God will bring a people whom He loves and who love Him, who are humble toward the faithful and disdainful toward the truth-concealers, who struggle in the path of God and fear not the blame of any blamer. That is God's bounty-He gives it to whom-soever He will. He is All-embracing, All-knowing (5:54).*

> *And if ye turn away, He will exchange you for other folk, and they will not be the likes of you (47:38).*

We are, therefore, asking God to guide us to the same straight path that He had shown to all those individuals who earned His

Sixth Verse: The Path of Those Whom Thou Hast Favored 69

grace, favor, and blessings. The Quranic term for these wholesome people is *salihun*. In the Quran among the *salihun* are the prophets. But any sincere and devoted Muslim who continuously strives to achieve *taqwa* can hope to join that group: *"And as for those who have faith and do wholesome deeds, We shall surely admit them among the wholesome"* (29:9). And in the following verse, the Quran clearly identifies four types of people whom God has blessed.

Whoso obeyeth God and the messenger, they are those unto whom God has shown favor, of the Prophets, and the saints, and the martyrs, and the righteous. The best of company are they! (4:69).

Seventh Verse:
Not (the Path) of Those Who Earn Thine Anger Nor of Those Who Go Astray

We are praying that through God's grace and mercy, we will follow the path of those who have earned His grace, and not of those who incurred God's wrath or condemnation, nor of those who went astray. Some commentators have suggested [based on a *hadith* from Tirmidhi] that those identified as incurring God's wrath are Jews, and those who went astray are Christians.

Even accepting the authenticity of this *hadith*, it only means that the Prophet mentioned these groups as examples and did not in any way mean to exclude other groups. In what category would one place the group of Meccan pagans who bitterly opposed the Prophet and continued to wage war for almost sixteen years? We cannot rigidly stick to this interpretation especially since both Jews and Christians were treated as *"ahl-al-kitab"* [People of the Book] and in many respects were given a special status:

> *The food of the People of the Book is lawful unto you, and yours is lawful unto them. (Lawful unto you in marriage) Are (not only) chaste women who are believers, but chaste women among the people of the book (5:5).*

One of the chief characteristics of the Noble Quran is that, though in a particular context or situation the Quran makes a negative or positive statement about certain people, it does not, in general, reprove or exonerate any individual or nation unconditionally. The Quran teaches that God, the Lord of mankind, does not favor any individual or nation. Individuals as well as communities will be judged on the basis of piety and righteousness. The following verses make this point unmistakably clear:

> Lo! Those who believe (in that which is revealed unto thee) and those who are Jews, and Christians, and Sabaeans-whoever believeth in God and the Last Day and doth right-surely their reward is with their Lord, and there shall no fear come upon them neither shall they grieve (2:62; cf 5:69).

Therefore, the two categories of people identified in the seventh verse of *surah al-fatihah* have to be explained in much broader terms: first, those who incur God's wrath, which refers to that group of people who, due to moral perversion, deliberately and wilfully break God's command and brazenly reject the truth, and second, those who go astray, which refers to those who show moral apathy and are so careless and negligent that they fail to recognize the truth. This may be in conformity with a hadith which explains the three essential tendencies of man. "In speaking of these three tendencies the Prophet drew a cross: the 'straight way' is the ascending vertical; the 'divine wrath' acts in the opposite direction, and the dispersion of 'those who stray' is in the horizontal direction."

When a struggle begins between "truth" [*haqq*] and "falsehood" [*batil*] and as it deepens, usually three types of people emerge. One group recognizes the "truth" and is ready to support the just cause with all their resources regardless of the consequences. The second group of people recognize the "truth" and righteous ways, but are too weak to give any substantial support.

They, nevertheless, may sympathize with the cause. The third group is of those people who are so wicked and hardhearted that they exhibit a complete distortion of moral values. They not only do bad and sinful things, but show brazen attitude, and mistakenly believe or somehow become convinced that what they are doing is good. In the forefront, they fiercely oppose the just and righteous cause and do not hesitate to commit all their resources to fight it to the finish. This group consists of rebellious and wicked people spreading corruption on Earth [*fasad fil-ard*]:

> *When it is said to them, 'Make not mischief on earth.' They say, 'We are only ones that put things right.' Of a surety, they make mischief, but they realize (it) not* (2:10-12).

> *His aim everywhere is to spread mischief through the earth and destroy crops and progeny, but God loveth not mischief.* (2:205)

> *And to those who are rebellious and wicked, their abode will be the Fire* (32:20).

> *For they are people rebellious in transgression* (27:12).

The best examples of this group are Meccan pagans and the hypocrites [*munafiqun*] of Medina. They did every thing destructive in their power to destroy both the message and the messenger. Nevertheless, Islam, the religion of "truth," finally prevailed. Consequently, after the conquest of Mecca, when the Prophet entered the Kabah, he repeated the following verse of the Quran:

> *Truth hath come and falsehood hath vanished; for falsehood is (by its nature) bound to vanish* (17:81).

The Quran introduces a completely new idea in trying to

explain the behavior of those who are continuously engaged in an aggressive and destructive behavior. It points out that those who are evil doers are actually engaged in an aggressive campaign against their own "selves." They are, therefore, committing an act of aggression against their own "*nafs*"—in Quranic terminology it is called "*zulm al-nafs*" [self-injustice]. According to the Quran all injustice is basically reflexive: all evil, all injustice, all harm that one does to someone else one ultimately does to oneself.

> *We wronged them not, but they did wrong themselves* (2:57).

> *They said: our Lord! We have wronged ourselves* (7:23).

> *God wronged them not, but they did wrong themselves* (3:117).

> *My Lord! Lo! I have wronged my soul, so forgive me. Then He forgave him* (28:16).

This theme is constantly repeated in the Quran: that individuals, by doing injustice to others, do injustice to their own souls.

> *It was not we wronged them; they wronged their own souls* (11:101).

> *Not God who wrongs them, But they wrong their own souls* (9:70).

> *(But they rebelled) to us, they did no harm, but they harmed their own souls* (7:160).

> *And whoso transgresseth God's limits, He verily wrongeth his soul* (65:1).

One major cause of this malaise is man's pettiness and selfishness. His pride, arrogance, and egotistical behavior finally becomes self-destructive. In this modern age, we are also witnessing the phenomenal rise of individualism. The new morality tends to glorify individual rights and assert that only the individual counts; the advancement of the individual is considered the be-all and end-all. When carried to its logical extreme, this enthronement of the individual completely undermines group norms and eventually leads to a kind of anarchy as an ideal.

The basic philosophy underlying new morality is: "I may do anything that does not hurt others; I am the boss of my own body and absolute owner of my own life." Now we are beginning to realize that our lack of ecological wisdom, combined with avaricious selfishness, prevented us from seeing that every action has its effects on others, farther along some ecological social chain. There is absolutely no human action that will affect only the performer or only other consenting adult. But modern man is surrounded by a life-style in which the pursuit of self-interest is glorified as the key to progress.

Arrogance, selfishness, and greed usually permeate man's overall behavior, which results in flagrant denial and violation of other people's rights. The Quran warns against social injustice, oppression of the poor and weak, and barriers between man and man.

> *God enjoins justice, kindness and charity to one's kindred, and forbids indecency, wickedness and oppression. He admonishes you so that you may take heed* (16:90).

The human being is so absorbed in his selfish, narrow, and material concerns, that he does not heed the ends of life [al-akhira]. The Quran, therefore, never ceases to warn the human being that this craze for wealth, power, and high status accompanied by a niggardly attitude will lead to everlasting punishment:

> *Truly the human being was created very impatient-Fretful [in a state of panic] when evil touches him; and niggardly when Good reaches him (70:19-21).*
>
> *The human being's souls are swayed by greed (4:128).*
>
> *The successful are those who can be saved from their own selfishness (59:9; 64:16).*
>
> *He was not believing God Almighty, nor urging to feed the destitute; today he has no friend here (69:33-35).*

In another passage, the Quran says that hell-fire: *...calls him who backs out and withdraws, and amasses and hoards* (70:17).

Just like the modern human being, "it was in supereminent wealth that the Meccans found the meaning of life. Wealth gave them power, and to increase one's wealth became the great aim in life"[31] The Quran, therefore, issues a stern warning against this obsession with worldly goods and riches:

> *And there are those who buy gold and silver and spend not in the Way of God: announce to them a most grievous penalty-On the Day when heat will be produced out of that (wealth) in the fire of Hell, and with it will be branded their foreheads, their flanks, and their backs. 'This is the (treasure) which ye buried for yourself: taste ye, then the (treasure) ye buried! (9: 34-35).*
>
> *And let not those who covetously withhold of the gifts which God hath given them of His Grace, think that it is good for them: Nay, it will be worse for them: soon shall the things which they covetously withheld be tied to their necks like a twisted collar, on the Day of Judgement (3:180).*

Seventh Verse: Not (the Path) of Those Who Earn Thine Anger... 77

> *Competition in accumulating wealth keeps you preoccupied until you visit your graves (102:1-2).*
>
> *But he who is greedy miser and thinks himself self-sufficient, and We will indeed make smooth for him the path to misery; Nor will his wealth profit him when he falls headlong (into the pit) (92:8-11).*

The Quran regards "pride in wealth" [*isthighna*] as the root of the social malaise underlying materialistic society. In other words the Quran looks upon a man's life as meaningful and successful when it is "upright" [*hanif*]. The supreme aim in life is not to live a life of pleasure and increase one's wealth and power, but to live "uprightly." The man who pursues wealth unscrupulously is characterized by the Quran as "niggardly." And many *ahadith* (Traditions) paint a graphic picture of the punishment awaiting the niggardly offender on the Day of Judgement. By making "niggardliness" a serious sin, the Quran is clearly showing the incompatibility between the worship of one God and the worship of wealth and power.

We are therefore asking God's help to prevent us from following a wrong course and seeking His guidance to lead us to the path of those upon whom He has bestowed His blessings. However, only through God's grace and mercy can one attain piety and righteousness. Consequently, we have been asked to pray:

> *Our Lord! Condemn us not if we forget, or miss the mark! Our Lord! Lay not on us such a burden as Thou didst lay on those before us! Our Lord! Impose not on us that which we have not the strength to bear! Pardon us, absolve us, and have mercy on us! Thou art our Protector... (2:286).*

NOTES

1 Edward Gibbon, *The Decline amd Fall of the Roman Empire*, Vol. 3, p.82

2 Alfred Guillaume, *Islam*, p.68.

3 Watchtower: *Mankind's Search for God*.

4 Sachiko Murata and William C. Chittick, *The Vision of Islam* pp. 46-47.

5 Huston Smith, *The Religions of Man*, p. 303.

6 Karen Armstrong, *A History of God*, p.117

7 Jules Masserman, *Time Magazine*, July 15, 1974.

8 Michael H. Hart, *The One Hundred*, pp. 33-40.

9 Karen Armstrong, *Muhammad: A Biography of the Prophet*, p. 93

10 John Esposito, *Islam, The Straight Path*, p.28

11 *The Vision of Islam, op. cit.*, p. 279.

12 Tertullian, *On Female Dress*, I, i.

13 Abu Ala 'l-Mawdudi, *Tafhim al-quran*, Vol.2, p. 189.

14 *Spirit of Islam, op. cit..*, p 184.

15 *Ibid.*, p 165.

16 Herbert Benson, "Psychological factors in healing: a new perspective on an old debate," pp. 5-11

17 David Larson, "A Measure of religiousness and its relation to parent child mental health variables," pp. 34-43.

18 Jeffrey Levin, "Religion and health: is there an association, and is it valid, and is it casual?" pp. 1475-1482.

19 *Time Magazine*, June 24, 1996.

20 Syed Sulaiman Nadvi, *Sirat al-Nabi*, Vol.3 pp. 466-467.

21 Muhammad Hamidullah, *Muhammad Rasulullah*, pp. 51-52.
22 Arthur Koestler, *The Ghost in the Machine.*
23 *Sirat al-Nabi, op. cit.,* Vol. 5, p 311.
24 Fazlur Rahman, *Major Themes of the Quran*, p.11
25 *Ibid.*, p.127-128.
26 *A History of God, op. cit.,* p. 151
27 *Ibid.*, p. 151-152
28 Martin Lings, *Muhammad: his Life Based on the Earliest Sources,* p. 324.
29 William Stoddart, *Sufism*, p. 82.
30 Muhammad Asad, *The Message of the Quran.*
31 Montgomery W. Watt, Muhammad: *The Prophet and Statesman*, p. 51.

BIBLIOGRAPHY

Ali, Syed Ameer. *The Spirit of Islam*, published in many editions—quotations used here are from that of Islamabad, Pakistan: National Book Foundation, 1981.

Armstrong, Karen. *Muhammad: A Biography of the Prophet*, San Francisco: Harper, 1993, p. 93

Armstrong, Karen, A History of God, Ballantine Books, N.Y. 1993.

Asad, Muhammad. *The Message of the Quran*. Dar al-Andalus Ltd., Gibralter: Dist. E. J. Brill, London 1980.

Benson, Herbert. "Psychological factors in healing :A New Perspective on an old Debate." *Journal of Behavioral Medicine*, Vol.18 (1) 1992) pp. 5-11

Esposito, John. *Islam: The Straight Path*, (Oxford university Press, 1988) p.28

Gibbon, Edward. *The Decline and Fall of the Roman Empire*, Vol. 3. Published in many editions—quotation used here is from that of NY: *The Modern Library*, undated.

Guillaume, Alfred. Islam. NY: Viking Penguin, 1954.

Hamidullah, Muhammad. *Muhammad Rasulullah*. Paris: Centre Cultural Islamique, 1974.

Hart, Michael H. *The One Hundred*. NY: Hart Publishing Co.Inc., 1978).

Koestler, Arthur. *The Ghost in the Machine*. London: Arkana/Penguin Books, 1989.

Larson, David. "A Measure of religiousness, and its relation to parent child mental health variables," *Journal of*

Community Psychology, Vol. 18 (1), 1990.

Levin, Jeffrey. "Religion and health: is there an association, and is it valid, and is it casual?" *Journal of Social Science and Medicine*, Vol. 38 (11), 1994.

Lings, Martin. *Muhammad: His Life Based on the Earliest Sources*, Rochester, VT: Inner Traditions Ltd., 1983.

Masserman, Jules. Time Magazine, July 15, 1974.

Mawdudi, Abu 'l-Ala. *Tafhim al-quran*, Vol. 2. Lahore, Pakistan: Idarah Tajumanul-Quran, 1978.

Murata, Sachiko and Chittick, William C. *The Vision of Islam* NY: Paragon House, 1994.

Nadvi, Syed Sulaiman. *Sirat al-Nabi*, Vol.3. Published in many editions—quotations used here are from that of Islamabad, Pakistan: National Book Foundation, 1981.

Rahman, Fazlur. *Major Themes of the Quran*. Chicago: Bibliotheca Islamica, 1980.

Smith, Huston. *The Religions of Man* NY: Harper and Row Publishers, 1989.

Stoddart, William. *Sufism*. NY: Paragon House, rev. edition 1985.

Time Magazine, June 24, 1996.

Watchtower. *Mankind's Search for God*. NY: Bible and Tract Society, 1990.

Watt, Montgomery. W. *Muhammad: The Prophet and Statesman* NY: Oxford University Press, 1974.

General Index

abasa, 12
Abd al-Wahhab, 43, 45
Abd Allah ibn Umm al-Maktum, 12
Abd Allah, 7, 12
Abraham, 3, 28, 49, 57, 64, 66-67
Absolute, 4, 7, 15-16, 32, 75
Abu 'l-Ala Mawdudi, 44, 45
Adam, 13, 37-39, 57
Adi ibn Hatim, 43-44
ahadith, 4, 77
ahl al-kitab, 71
Ahriman, 14
Ahura Mazda, 14
al-akhira, 33, 75
al-amin, 24
al-hamd, 7
alam al-ghaib, 45
Ali ibn Abi Talib, 17
Allah, 7-9, 11-12, 34, 45, 66
aman, 67
anam, 7
Anselm, 14
Arabia, 7, 24-25
Arabs, 11,
Arius of Alexandria, 14
Armstrong, Karen, 25, 62, 79
arrogance, 39-40, 75
Aryans, 11
Asharite, 15
assas al-quran, 4
Augustine, St., 14, 38
Avesta, 1
Babel, 54
batil, 72
Baydawi, al-, 18
Bible, 37, 82
bismi ka allahumma, 17
bismi llahi al-rahman al-rahim, 17

Buddha, 51
Cherisher, 10, 41
Chittick, 8, 32, 79, 82
Christ, 37
Christian (s), 3, 5, 8-9, 14-15, 36-38, 43, 62-64, 67-68, 71-72
Christianity, 14, 23, 37, 43
Community, 11, 23-24, 27, 36, 45, 48, 58, 67, 82
Dartmouth-Hitchcock Medical Center, 51
Day of Decision, 29; of Reckoning, 29, 33; of Resurrection, 29, 35-36
De Trinitate, 14
din, 28-29, 65
Dispenser, 19
Eli, 8
Elohim, 8
Eloi, 8
Esposito, John, 27, 79, 81
Eternal, 2, 14-16, 29, 66
Eve, 38-39
Everlasting Refuge, 16, 40, 46
fadl Allah, 34
falsehood, 56, 72-73
Farewell Pilgrimage, 13
fasad fil-ard, 73
fatir, 7
Foundation of the Quran, 4, 7, 82
Gathas, 1
Ghafur, al-, 18
Gibbon, Edward, 1, 79
Guillaume, Alfred, 5, 79
hadith, 8, 43, 47, 71-72
hajj, 57
halal, 44

Hamidullah, 80-81
Hanafi, 44
Hanbali, 44
hanif, 77
haqq, 72
haram, 44
hasanat, 20
hidaya, 49
Hindus, 8
Hira, 9
Holy Spirit, 14
hubb, 19
huda li-nas, 21, 49
Hudaybiyyah, 17
huquq al-ibad, 11
huquq Allah, 11
hypocrisy, 32
hypocrites, 73
ibadah, 56
Iblis, 39
Ibn al-Arabi, 65
ikhlas, 32
imams, 44
Isaac, 64, 66-67
Ishmael, 64, 66-67
Israel, 11
isthighna, 77
istikbar, 39
Jacob, 64, 66
Jesus, 3, 8, 25, 28, 37, 49-51, 64, 66-67
Jews, 5, 8-9, 36, 43, 62-63, 67-68, 71-72
Judge, 10, 25, 27, 36-37
judgment, 4, 27-31, 33, 35-37, 39
jugular vein, 4, 18, 42, 46
Jurjani, al- 15
Just Judge, 27
Kabah, 25, 73
kahf, 7
khair, 34
kinz, al-, 4
Koestler, Arthur, 80

84 Index

Larson, David, 79
lawful, 44, 71
Lings, Martin, 64, 80
Lord's Prayer, 3-5, 7
love, 19-20, 22, 34, 39, 55, 65, 68
Malaki, 44
Masserman, Jules, 24, 79
Massignon, Louis, 15
Mecca, 1, 23-26, 73
Meccans, 12, 17, 26, 76
Medina, 24, 64, 73
Michael Hart, 24, 79, 81
miraj, al-, 52
monotheism, 3, 42
Moses, 1, 8, 21, 24, 28, 49, 51-52, 64, 66-67
Most Gracious, 4, 17-19, 21, 23, 25
Most Merciful, 4, 17-19, 21, 23, 25-26
mujtahids, 44
munafiqun, 73
Murata, Sacheko, 8, 32, 79, 82
Muslim mystics, 19
muttaqi, 56
Nadvi, Syed Sulaiman, 80
nafs, 74
nafy, 42
Nasruddin, 53
National Institute on Aging, 51
New Testament, 3, 14
Nicaea, 14
nifaq, 32
Noah, 28, 49
Old Testament, 3, 8
Orientalists, 23
original sin, 36-38
Patriarch, 3
Pentateuch, 1
People of the Book, 71
pilgrimage, 13, 57

polytheism, 41-42, 45-46
priests, 43-44, 46
Protector, 10, 19, 41, 77
Quraysh, 11, 17, 24-26
rabb al-alamin, 11
rabb, 9, 11
rabbis, 43-44, 46
rahim, 17-18
rahman, 17-18, 55, 80, 82
Rahman, Fazlur, 55
rahmat al-alamin, 22
ratamorphic, 54
Risalat al-ahadiyyah, 43
riya, 32
Rumi, 19
saba, 7
saban min al-mathani, 4
salih, 31
salihat, 32
salihun, 32, 69
Samad, al-, 15-16, 46
Satan, 39
sayyiat, 20
scientific myth, 53
scientific superstition, 53
Seven of the Oft-repeated, 4
Shafi'i, 44
Shah Wali Allah, 45
shahadah, 8, 42
shirk al-ibadah, 45
shirk al-ilm, 45
shirk al-tasarruf, 45
shirk, 13, 41-42, 45-48
sirah, 22
sirat al-mustaqim, 54
situation ethics, 53
slm, 66
Smith, Huston, 11, 79
Son, 14, 37-38, 66
straight path, 4, 49, 51, 53-55, 57, 59, 61, 68,

79, 81
Sufi(s), 19, 43, 53, 65
Supreme Being, 7, 13
surah al-ikhlas, 15
surah al-isra, 52
Sustainer, 10, 41
tahmid, 7
taqwa, 12, 54-59, 67, 69
tawhid, 42-43
Tawwab, al-, 18
temptress, 38-39
Ten Commandments, 51-52
Tertullian, 14, 38, 79
Thamud, 49
Tirmidhi, 71
Treasure, 4, 25, 76
Treatise on Oneness, 43
trimurti, 14
Trustworthy, 24
truth, 13, 27-28, 36, 53-54, 56, 65-66, 72-73
Twelve Commandments, 52
umm al-quran, 4
ummah, 48
Uncaused Cause, 16
Unity of Being, 43
Universal Brotherhood, 11, 51
unlawful, 44
Vishnu, 8
Wahdat al-wujud, 43
wholesome deeds, 31-32, 68-69
wholesome people, 32, 69
wqy, 55, 67
Yahweh, 2
yawm al-fasl, 29; *al-hisab*, 29; *al-qiyamah*, 29
Zeus, 8
Zoroaster, 1, 14
zulm al-nafs, 74